RELIGION IN
SOCIOLOGICAL PERSPECTIVE

RELIGION IN SOCIOLOGICAL PERSPECTIVE

BRYAN WILSON

OXFORD UNIVERSITY PRESS
OXFORD   NEW YORK

Oxford University Press, Walton Street, Oxford OX2 6DP

Oxford New York
Athens Auckland Bangkok Bombay
Calcutta Cape Town Dar es Salaam Delhi
Florence Hong Kong Istanbul Karachi
Kuala Lumpur Madras Madrid Melbourne
Mexico City Nairobi Paris Singapore
Taipei Tokyo Toronto

and associated companies in
Berlin Ibadan

Oxford is a trade mark of Oxford University Press

Published in the United States by
Oxford University Press Inc., New York

First published in 1982

British Library Cataloguing in Publication Data
Wilson, Bryan
Religion in sociological perspective.
1. Religion and sociology—Addresses, essays,
lectures
I. Title
306.'6   BL60
ISBN 0-19-826664-2 Pbk

9 10 8

Printed in Great Britain on acid-free paper by
Biddles Ltd, Guildford and King's Lynn

Preface

Sociology, in common with the other social and natural sciences, emerged as a product of western civilization. But whereas the natural sciences, and to a large extent economics, with its narrow commitment to a normative rationality, could readily surmount the cultural inhibitions and biases of their circumstances of origin and early development, sociology found it much less easy to transcend the social context in which it was evolved. Sociology was, so to say, infected by its own subject matter, by the assumptions and perspectives of the societies in which the so-called science of society was conceived and developed. Its generalizations were usually those that pertained to western societies, and its world-view was subtly dependent on the cultures in which sociologists themselves practised. Even when new subject matter was infused into this discipline from anthropology, all too often the theoretical propositions formulated in the study of tribal societies were applied, with only laggardly modifications to accommodate the differences of scale and complexity, to advanced western social systems. Other patterns of societal organization had to wait for proper sociological attention. The subject's commitment to abstract, universal propositions induced a premature and facile optimism concerning the extent to which sociology, representing itself as the social equivalent of physics, might embody one definitive body of high level theory. Its position was, none the less, deeply compromised by the indebtedness of sociological concepts to specifically western cultures, and this indebtedness—in so far as sociology persists with its early ideals—it has never quite transcended.

Yet, despite these evident limitations, the growing impact of western science and technology on non-western nations has steadily made the cultural captivity of the sociologist less significant. In technical, economic, and organizational matters, the rest of the world becomes progressively westernized, and although this does not immediately produce patterns of social relations or social structures that correspond to those of the West, increasingly western influences, mediated by these disciplines and techniques and their applications, influence social life throughout the world and in a wide variety of ways. The sociologist should be aware of, and should be interested in, the differences that persist, but he tends towards an implicit, if not always a confident, expectation that human societies will increasingly respond to the same imperatives in ultimately somewhat similar ways. Gradually, and just as sociologists were becoming aware of it and self-conscious about it, the culture-boundedness of sociology appears, at least superficially, to be of diminishing significance.

The sociologist of religion, however, if he has concerned himself at all with religious phenomena outside the confines of western Christendom, has been made more acutely aware of the radical differences among the world's societies. Religion retains the imprints of long-persisting cultural imperatives and deeply felt commitments, and this is true even of the religions that are generally designated as 'new', such as those that have become conspicuous throughout the world in the last three decades. The fundamental concepts of the sociology of religion have, since the subject's very beginnings, been heavily indebted to Christian theology, and their applicability to the religions of the non-Christian world has always been problematic. Only slowly, and then very unevenly, have the exponents of the discipline recognized and wrestled with the problems of re-shaping its conceptual frameworks to accommodate other world religions. The typical search by the theorists for universal generalizations was, to say no more, at least a premature exercise, carried forward by excessive enthusiasm for the none the less promising insights afforded from the general sociological perspective. That the promises were made in good faith and that much might be yielded to redeem them, I strongly believe; but it will not be at the level of abstract meta-theory of a world-encompassing kind.

The problems that I have adumbrated had occurred to me before, but my awareness of these considerations was very much heightened by the invitation that I received to deliver several lectures on specified themes in Tokyo in 1979. Those lectures are gathered in this volume. My academic audiences were, needless to say, men and women whose culture and religious background were radically different from those of any western audiences which might gather to listen to lectures in the sociology of religion. The need to reconsider basic concepts and to attempt to relate the discipline to a completely different religious environment was very much borne in upon me. I am grateful to those audiences for their forbearance, for their penetrating questions, and for their invariably gentle but usually cogent criticisms of what I had to say. My lectures were delivered under the sponsorship of the Oriental Institute of Philosophy and Soka University (excepting only the last essay in this volume, which is a subject on which I have spoken in various places in a variety of somewhat different presentations). I should like to take this opportunity to thank, among others, Mr Ryuichi Goto of the Oriental Institute of Philosophy for the organization of the lectures, and for his valuable comments on them, and Dr Kazuo Takamatsu, President of Soka University, for his kindness and courtesy in the arrangements made for me to speak at Soka University. I have a special debt to Mr Tsuyoshi Nakano who has translated these lectures into Japanese, and who, in the course of his work, very much assisted my own thinking by drawing to my attention inconsistencies and obscurities in my text; for any which remain, I am of course solely responsible.

Contents

I

The Sociology of Religion
as a Science

The significance of religion to sociology
From the very beginning of the development of sociology,
religion was recognized to be a social phenomenon of the utmost
importance. It would not perhaps be too much to say that the
founders of sociology, Auguste Comte and, in some measure, his
immediate predecessor, Henri Saint-Simon, saw the new
science, which Comte designated 'sociology', as a replacement
of the theological interpretation of social phenomena. Before
the new science arose, theology, or at a more popular level,
religion, had been the inevitable, albeit erroneous, basis for
man's comprehension of society (and, indeed, of nature). For
Comte, the most complete expression of religion was, of course,
Christianity, and, more specifically, Roman Catholicism. In
that tradition, the total environment had been not merely
viewed religiously (for that occurred even in primitive religion)
but also elaborately explained in terms that made God the
central point of reference. From God stemmed the cosmos and
the natural order, and the social and moral order. Christianity
had canvassed a God-centred understanding of creation. God
had created the earth, and the earth was the centre of the cosmic
stage, for the benefit of which (and more specifically for the
benefit of mankind), the sun, moon, and stars had been
specifically created. Man was the pinnacle of God's creation,
and man's affairs, his history, his corruption and his redemp-
tion, were the central preoccupations of religious faith: man's
history was the outworking of God's providence. Within the
framework of this theological scheme, God's will, man's duty,
the social fabric, and the conduct of social relationships were all
encompassed. Christian theology, then, had been a rudimen-
tary explanation and legitimation of the social system. In the
context of what purported to be fact, were embraced the

prescriptions and injunctions that rested on a fundamental system of value-judgements; and at the centre of it all was God.

It was the undermining of the old religious conception of the natural order that permitted the attempt of the early sociologists to put forward an alternative to the theological conception of the social order—and indeed to suggest that, in the past, man had necessarily been committed to a religious *Weltanschauung*. God was now divested of his central position in social and moral concerns: human affairs were to be ordered no longer for God's pleasure but solely for man's welfare. Science was to be recognized as a system of human knowledge, and knowledge must be empirical and positivist. In Comte's formulation, the way in which man perceived the world was the basis on which social organization rested. As man's way of perceiving the world changed from the theological to the positivistic perspective, so the social order would also change.[1]

To divest theology of its claim to be the fundamental discipline and queen of the sciences was, despite the increasing independence of the natural sciences, not easy in the social realm. To describe his new science of morals and politics, Saint-Simon had to resort to the designation 'the new Christianity' in order to convey the idea that, different as were his premisses, none the less, his concerns were similar to those rooted in religious ideas of society and morality. How were the deep-laid and implicitly religious elements of interpretation to be discarded whilst retaining the fundamental concern with issues and subject matter which had, hitherto, been conceivable only in religious terms? Clearly, the new science of society was to be built on the model of older (natural) sciences, even though it was to concern itself with the subject-matter of religion and the humanities. The process which Comte discerned in history, a process of changing human consciousness, must now be made self-conscious: men must be brought to an awareness of how their view of the world had changed, and this knowledge in itself would lead to the acceleration of this process and so bring men to a conscious positivism. From primitive fetishism to modern science was the process that Comte sought to make evident. It

---

[1] Comte's thought is set out in his *Cours de philosophie positive* 1830–42. Still a useful introduction is John Stuart Mill, *Auguste Comte and Positivism* (1865), Ann Arbor: University of Michigan Press, 1961. See also, E. E. Evans-Pritchard, *The Sociology of Comte: An Appreciation*, Manchester: Manchester University Press, 1970.

had occurred in the natural sciences, and it must now follow in the social sciences. In the new science of society, sociology, factual observation, detached, objective, empiricism would displace metaphysical speculation. Sociology would be as neutral as physics. Ultimate questions would be abandoned as meaningless, and knowledge would take human welfare as its final concern. Humanity was to be deity, and altruism the rule of life.

The position adopted by Comte towards religion did not, of course, continue to be the exclusive orientation of sociology. But it has been necessary to recall Comte's perspective since it reveals the sources of tension between the claims of sociology (and hence of the sociology of religion) to be scientific when confronting a *Weltanschauung* that is patently normative, arbitrary, and metaphysical, and which exploits the mythical, the ritualistic, and the emotional. In this stark contrast of orientations, repose some of the continuing difficulties of the sociology of religion. But precisely because religion had, in the pre-scientific ages, been so central to both social organization and human consciousness, and because it was now so strongly the focus of challenge—first in the very assumption that society could be organized on, and human consciousness informed by, other principles; and second in the contrast of methodology that sociology presented to religion—so religion has remained of much more importance to sociological enquiry than any other institutional area of society.

Subsequent sociologists did not escape involvement in the issues raised by Comte's programme for the replacement of religion by positivist sociology. His immediate successors were less stridently positivisitic, but the goal of self-direction for society remained in the writings of Herbert Spencer and L. T. Hobhouse, with industrial development as its principal facilitating agency.[2] In America—a self-constituted new society in which optimism and faith in an improving social order was fed by buoyant expansion—the ideological thrust of sociology against religion was muted. There, indeed, sociology was used as a prop for the social gospel, and religious voluntarism became in itself almost an evidence of commitment to social good in the

[2] See Herbert Spencer, *First Principles*, London, rev. edn. 1900; and idem, *The Principles of Sociology*, London, 1885–96; L. T. Hobhouse, *Morals in Evolution* (1915), London, Chapman and Hall, 7th edn., 1951; idem, *Social Development*, London, 1924.

sociological sense. Much as the practical positivism of Comte was consonant with American pragmatism, his ideological rejection of religion was usually ignored. The theoretical implications for religion of Comtean sociology were not squarely faced, even though Comte's ideas were taught in some American universities, and even though sociology became institutionally established there long before any such development occurred in Europe. Outside the universities, however, critical sociological thinking steadily developed and progressed in Europe, and since, in European countries, religion was officially endorsed, critical and dissenting attitudes towards the churches flourished among the intellectuals. The scientific attitude was acceptable not only in practice (as in America) but also in theory, and what Peter Berger has called 'methodological atheism' was embraced as the appropriate posture of sociologists towards religion. Such a stance is evident in the work of Karl Marx and Sigmund Freud. For each of them, religion was to be not only explained, but also to be 'explained away'. For Marx, religion was mystification, a manifestation of false consciousness, to be explained as a search by men for compensation in their mistery, and as an agency of social control deployed by the ruling classes in the class struggle. For Freud, religion was an institutionalized mass neurosis. Even though he acknowledged that designating it as such would do nothing to relieve man of his irrational psychological dispositions, by therapy men might realize the nature of their dependence on the illusory quality of religious fictions, which they had constructed for their own self-protection. Marx, concerned with his own science of society, said little of the mystification that Marxism was expected to disperse, but Freud, whenever he turned from his clinical cases to an analysis of society, turned recurrently to an extended discussion of religion. Religion was a key issue in understanding social and human consciousness, and their pathologies.[3]

[3] The references to religion in the writings of Karl Marx and Friedrich Engels are numerous, often fragmentary, and dispersed; the reader is advised to consult the index of their collected works. Freud's work on religion is also widely diffused through his work, but see especially, Sigmund Freud, *The Future of an Illusion*, London: Standard Edn., 1953–74, Vol. XXI; idem, *Civilization and its Discontents*, XXI; idem, *Moses and Monotheism*, XXIII. For a general commentary, see Philip Rieff, *Freud: The Mind of the Moralist*, London: Gollancz, 1959; and idem, *The Triumph of the Therapeutic: The Uses of Faith after Freud*, London: Chatto and Windus, 1966. For a contemporary application of psychoanalytic insight into religion, see C. R. Badcock, *The Psychoanalysis of Culture*, Oxford: Blackwell, 1980.

Within the Comtean, Marxist, and Freudian approaches to religion there was contained an unresolved issue of tension. All three writers, together with those who later claimed to adopt the same intellectual positions, sought to be scientific in their analysis of society: the science of society was the watchword of both Comte and Marx. Science implied detachment, objectivity, and ethical neutrality; for Comte and his successors, this was indeed the vital feature of sociology. Yet in all these traditions the science of society was regarded as emerging in order to dislodge the religious conceptions of man and the world by which mankind had previously governed social affairs. Thus there persisted a certain animus against religion, whilst, at the same time, the claim was made that sociologists viewed society with detachment and according to the canons of value-freedom. Thus, sociology was in its nature set over against a religious world-view, in which cognitive, evaluative, and affective elements were inevitably intertwined. Sociology sharply pointed out the defectiveness of an orientation which not only purported to describe the facts of the world and its order, but which simultaneously prescribed the attitudes, feelings, and evaluations with which man should regard those supposed 'facts'. By its very detachment and objectivity, sociology offered an alternative scientific view. Yet, we may ask, how was that scientific stance to be sustained: how might sociology maintain a neutral attitude towards religion when, at the same time, it sought to discredit it?

This issue of tension in the sociology of religion has never been entirely dispelled, even though as sociologists became more circumspect in their claims, and as they came increasingly to document the decline of religion as a purely sociological process (and not as a declaration of a sociological manifesto), so they ceased to present sociology as itself an alternative source of prescription for social order. Yet, since this stance had been so emphatic in Comte's work, sociology was from the beginning engaged with the question of religion. Later sociologists, even if completely free from the Comtean vision of an applied science of society, none the less necessarily needed to explain the role of religion in society, and the causes and circumstances of the changes in that role. To comprehend the nature of social development, sociologists needed to interpret the functions of religion in societies of the past.

Thus the classical sociologists of the early twentieth century were as much preoccupied with the sociology of religion as Comte had been. Max Weber in his attempt to explain the reasons for the development of western rationality, and of capitalism, the economic system which so completely embraced the principles of formal rationality, turned to religion as the source of value-systems that determine social organization. To religion he ascribed a powerful role in social development, even though he believed that religion was no longer the sustaining force of western economic and social order. If Weber is the most distinguished among sociologists, he is so largely because of the subtlety of his analysis of religion.[4] Much the same point might be made of Emile Durkheim, whose distinction as a sociologist is second only to that of Weber. We owe to him the pioneer analysis of the latent functions which religion fulfilled for society.[5] But Durkheim did not believe that in the future, religion would fulfil the functions that he had ascribed to it in primitive aboriginal Australian societies. In the modern world, religion was virtually defunct, and if its important functions were to be fulfilled, then, he believed, other agencies would be required to subserve them. He looked in turn to various social institutions, and came to believe that only the school and professional associations—restored to something like the form of mediaeval guild organizations—could establish normative consensus in modern, complex industrial society with its elaborate division of labour. In many ways, Durkheim's life work was an exploration in search of rational structures to supply the latent functions that had, in pre-literate societies, been fulfilled by religion. He sought by rational means to define agencies that would provide consciously all the erstwhile *un*intended consequences—the latent functions—of the ir-rational. Implicit in his analysis was the assumption that advanced society was becoming increasingly rational in its organization, and this must lead to the diminution of the influence of religion. At the same time, Durkheim believed

---

[4] Max Weber's works have been translated into English in various versions. The most important items for this discussion are *Wirtschaft und Gessellschaft*, Tübingen, Mohr, 2nd edn. 1925, and the *Gesammelte Aufsätze zur Religionssoziologie*, Tubingen: Mohr, 1920–1.

[5] Emile Durkheim, *The Elementary Forms of the Religious Life* (1912), (translated by J. W. Swain), Glencoe, Ill.: The Free Press, 1954; a useful compilation is W. S. F. Pickering, *Durkheim on Religion*, London; Routledge, 1975; see also Steven Lukes, *Emile Durkheim: His Life and Work*, London: Allen Lane The Penguin Press, 1973.

that society needed agencies that subserved consensus, and these had, in the past, been supplied by religion. It had provided the over-arching values and the normative order by which society was rendered cohesive. The new agencies that must be found to fulfil what he took to be indispensable functions, would, of necessity, be *consciously* instituted to this end. Thus, the course of social development was the process by which latent functions were made into manifest functions and since they were manifest they must therefore become the object of conscious and deliberate planning. Although Durkheim's thought went far beyond that of Comte, there is here, none the less, and even if expressed in a somewhat different way, Comte's old assumption that sociology might itself become the body of knowledge which informed social organization and social planning. Sociology was still seen as the exemplification of a self-consciously rational interpretation of social life, which was destined, both as part of social evolution and by virtue of the more developed conscious-ness about social organization, to displace religion as the source of values. Society would discover, or rather create, a rational ethic.

Clearly, even among the functionalists, who were disposed to make explicit the positive value of religion for society, the tension to which we have already alluded, between sociology's claim to a strict scientific stance of ethical neutrality, and its virtual 'take-over bid' of religion's erstwhile functions, con-tinued to exist. Among Durkheim's functionalist successors, for example Kingsley Davis, the view prevailed that whilst religion had been a useful fiction for society (and might to some extent continue as a useful fiction), there was a self-evident disjunction between what was good and what was true. For him religion was patently false; it persisted because it was socially valuable.[6]

Functionalism remains one of the dominant perspectives of sociology, and it has had a special appeal for sociologists of religion since it provides, by exposing latent functions, a basis for explaining the persistence of the non-rational facets of social life.[7] Functionalism 'makes sense' of arbitrary, empirically-

[6] See Kingsley Davis, *Human Society*, New York: Macmillan, 1948, especially pp. 509–48.

[7] On functionalism, see among other items, Kingsley Davis, 'The Myth of Functional Analysis as a Special Method in Sociology and Anthropology', *American Sociological Review*, 24 (1959), pp. 757–73; Robert K. Merton, *Social Theory and Social Structure*, Glencoe, Ill.: The Free Press, revd. edn. 1957, esp. pp. 20–84; and Llewellyn Gross (ed.), *Symposium on Sociological Theory*, Evanston, Ill.: Row Peterson, 1959, especially pp. 241–307; W. W. Isajiw, *Causation and Functionalism in Sociology*, London: Routledge, 1968.

unprovable teachings (myths), and of the persistence of equally arbitrary prescribed practices (rituals). Not all functionalists endorse the view of Davis that religion is a useful fiction: for some, the utility of religion to society might be taken as the basis of its justifiction; but for many, functionalism accounts for the apparently arbitrary, and certainly diverse, bodies of religious theory, belief and practice, for each single traditional corpus of which the claim is made that it is true (and sometimes that it is uniquely true). Yet it must also be acknowledged that sociologists of other schools, who explain religion by reference to its social provenance and distribution, embrace theories that may also imply that religious phenomena may be 'explained away'. Thus, Charles Y. Glock, who has developed the *relative deprivation thesis*, sees religion as virtually a compensatory response of deprived people. The response is likely to be differentially manifested according to the measure and kind of deprivation felt by specific groups within the total population. Those with the strongest sense of deprivation (relative to the facilities or competences enjoyed by others, or relative to their own earlier expectations of their own future prospects) were the most likely, according to this thesis, to embrace religion (or to embrace it more intensely)—and religion of a type calculated to compensate them for the specific sort of deprivation from which they suffered (or from which they believed themselves to suffer).[8]

The classical sociological authors came near to saying that men had evolved religion as a way of explaining things to themselves, just as Durkheim suggested that the concept of deity was an unconscious attempt to represent, and to objectify in symbolic terms, society to itself. They believed that with the dissociation of facts from values, and with the growth of empirical science and its objective techniques, religion would no longer be able to fulfil its earlier social functions. At the intellectual level, religious accounts of man, his world, and his prospects were shown to be deficient by the superior techniques of science. At the evaluative level, some of the earlier sociologists made their own assumptions about the future source of social

[8] See, for the early statement of this thesis, Charles Y. Glock, 'The Role of Deprivation in the Origin and Evolution of Religious Groups', in Robert Lee and Martin E. Marty (eds.), *Religion and Social Conflict*, New York: Oxford University Press, 1964, pp. 24–36, and for its implementation in research, C. Y. Glock, B. B. Ringer, and E. R. Babbie, *To Comfort and to Challenge*, Berkeley: University of California Press, 1967.

values. Some of them, elaborating their own codes, openly incorporated (like Hobhouse) or covertly smuggled (perhaps like Durkheim) a rational ethic into the projection of society's (and sociology's) future order.

At the emotional level, where this became an explicit concern, it was assumed that here, too, reason would itself come to master the passions, that in place of the techniques of socialization prompted by religious systems (which were effective but which were based on erroneous assumptions) would be created patterns of socialization that rested on reason or therapy. The 'reason' invoked was the logic of history for a Marx; the conscious accretion of affectivity to self-conscious conceptions of duty, as in Durkheim; and therapy was, of course, the one possibility of escape from the impasse that was allowed by Freudian theory. Weber alone left these issues poised on the knife-edge of his own acute and sensitive ambivalence, implying that modern man could no longer (intellectually) live with religion, whilst acknowledging that it was far from clear— once in the grip of the irrationalities of formal rationality— that he could live without it.

Yet, despite all of this, it must be clear that religion was a subject at the heart of classical sociological theory, and it remains true today that it continues to be at the core of the discipline. Since religion has been regarded by the sociologists as a 'pre-sociological' theory of society, then the sociology of religion as such must inevitably be a discipline in which central epistemological questions are at issue. And even though these concerns do not always become evident in, for instance, the sometimes unduly positivistic procedures of contemporary empirical sociologists of religion, they remain as the philosophical background of any interpretative statement about culture, knowledge, socialization, meaning, order—indeed of all the central questions of sociology *per se*.

Religion is not merely (and not necessarily primarily) an intellectual statement of the prerequisites of social order. It fulfilled its functions for society by summoning evaluative and affective dispositions, and by diffusing appropriate motivations, so encompassing a very wide range of human experience. It had affinities with art and poetry and the whole imaginative, creative realm of man's being. It simulated, channelled, and regulated, basic human emotions. It elicited sympathy, altruism, and love, intimating minute and often subtle desiderata that have shaped human comportment. The sociologist is necessarily concerned with such matters as social control, social consensus, the evocation of goodwill in human relations, and the maintenance of an appropriate balance in the expression of human emotions. All of these things have, in greater or lesser degree, been focused in religious activity, and religions have generally prescribed the evaluations that men should endorse towards various facets of their human experience. Whilst the higher religions at their most elevated and philosophical levels may provide a set of intellectual propositions that answer (in the religion's own terms—which are not terms that need convince an outsider) 'ultimate questions', practical religion, religion at the everyday level, has been preoccupied with other issues. Ultimate answers may indeed be an unimportant part of the functions of religion in many societies, and even in other societies, these ultimate concerns may be of limited consequence in the everyday life circumstances of those who, nominally, embrace the teachings of one of the higher religions. The social significance of religion has rather lain in the provision of categories and symbols that facilitate simultaneously man's comprehension of his circumstances and his capacity to evaluate them and to cope with them emotionally. Thus it is that religious language, unlike scientific language, is often highly ambiguous, seeking to denote and to evoke simultaneously, providing not only descriptions but also evaluations and summoning and sustaining particular types of emotional response. Religious language is at once a repertoire of supposedly objective categories, a storehouse of values, and a battery of manipulative symbols.

Sociology sought—and still seeks—to explain religion, and to do so in essentially scientific terms. The sociologist's interest in values is to regard them as data; other men's values are the sociologist's facts. Even though later sociologists were less sanguine than Comte, Hobhouse, and even Durkheim, that sociology would in the future be able to square the circle by providing a strictly rational basis for values, none the less values, including intimations of the supernatural, metaphysical speculations and ideas, emotional orientations, beliefs, rituals, and patterns of religious socialization and organization, were to be the subject of scientific, sociological enquiry.

Sociology as science

The foregoing remarks have sought to establish in some measure the significance of religion as an appropriate—indeed unavoidable—concern for sociology. But clearly, much as sociology as a scientific discipline must be explicitly committed to the maintenance of an adequate body of theory, increasingly sociologists have sought to test elements of theory, and to provide evidence that leads to confirmation or revision. As the facilities for social investigation have improved, both with the development of techniques of enquiry, and with the establishment of university positions from which sociologists might engage in research, so the sociological interest in religion has found increasingly empirical expression. Today, even though the theoretical issues remain important to the sociologist of religion, increasingly the test of the discipline is not in its broad theoretical (and often—it may be admitted—speculative) generalizations, but in the work that is done in the field.

In his field-work, the sociologist of religion is necessarily committed to the same type of scientific procedures that are employed by sociologists in any field. If by a science we mean a discipline in which empirical phenomena are investigated by methods of enquiry that are objective, in which the investigator attempts to maintain a distinct and self-conscious ethical neutrality, in which detachment from the data is maintained, and standard methods of measurement are used, then sociology may be said to be scientific. We may go further and suggest that a science is also characterized by the attempt to develop a rational body of theory in which individual phenomena are related to propositions of greater generality that are described in abstract conceptual language. Concepts are themselves formulations that facilitate the expression and co-ordination of hypothetical propositions which are, in principle, falsifiable. Such propositions may then be tested against empirical data.

In some measure, sociology meets these demands, and certainly these prescriptions have been the model for the development of the discipline. They apply no less to the sociology of religion. Of course, if by science is meant a procedure by controlled experiment, it is clear that sociology is limited in the extent to which it can utilize the techniques of the natural sciences. Not only are there practical difficulties, which I need not discuss, but the whole discipline here meets an ethical barrier which is not merely incidental to this discussion. The ethical barrier indicates the persistence of a sense of human integrity, of the individual's freedom of will, and of society's rights to operate without undue interference from the operation of social scientists. This ethical barrier should alert us to the fact that, in this respect, sociology appears to be in a position different in kind from at least the physical sciences, and different in considerable degree (if not in kind) from the biological sciences. The ethical barrier to the development of strictly scientific procedures in sociology intimates a limitation which the data impose upon the investigators, or, better, which the world imposes on the collection of data. It is a limitation which in itself probably suggests the boundaries beyond which scientific enquiry cannot go—not because the procedures are impossible, but because we have strong ethical objections to their use. This fact alone intimates the persistence of a significant, perhaps irreducible, value-commitment which suggests that values cannot be entirely explained scientifically, if for no other reason than because we will not allow them to be so explained. At this point the expansion of science meets human resistance, and perhaps here we have an intimation of a possible analogous limitation to the procedures of science in other spheres.

This issue aside, however, the sociology of religion is committed, as is any branch of sociology, to the maintenance of a scientific orientation. In this respect it becomes important to recognize just what the sociology of religion seeks to do, and what lies beyond its range of possibilities. In the first place, the sociology of religion takes the formulations of a religious movement, or the religious dispositions of a people, as its points of departure. The statement of beliefs, the prescriptions of ritual, and their basis of legitimation, are all taken as basic data—as phenomena existent at the emergent level from which the sociology of religion must proceed. The sociologist is not concerned to test the 'truth' of belief. He is not concerned with the efficacy of rituals. He does not attempt to judge between divergent interpretations of a tradition. He does not challenge the claimed legitimation for practices and ideas which religionists endorse. All of these things he must accept as part of the data. He proceeds at the emergent social level, with a body of information that must, in the first instance, come from the believers themselves. Whether his interest is in the nature of religious belief, in the appeal of religious teachings or rituals, in the processes of conversion, in the character of organization, the regularity of religious practice, the consequences of becoming religiously committed, the relation of priests to laymen, the style and function of religious legitimation, or whatever else it may be, the sociologist must first take the self-interpretation of religious individuals and groups as the point of departure from which his study begins. He does not, of course, seek to learn the doctrines of a religion in the same way in which believers seek to learn. He is not going to become a disciple. Were he to do so, he would necessarily cease to be a sociologist. But he should at least seek to understand exactly what it is that a disciple learns, and as far as possible he should seek to understand what *they* understand and should do so in *their* terms. Now clearly, since he is to remain detached and apart, there will inevitably be a gap between the ultimate meaning for him, and the meaning for the believer, of the same formulations. But he can, and indeed must, seek to acquire an empathic understanding of *their* commitment and *their* beliefs. Only if he can gain some apprehension of what it means to be a believer can he say anything useful about the religious movement he studies; and yet, in gaining that understanding, he must not actually become a believer.[9]

It will be apparent that the cultivation of what I call 'sympathetic detachment' will always remain a matter of difficulty, and between sympathy and detachment there is a frontier of tension. Mixing with a religious group, a sociologist may feel deeply drawn to them and to their activities, and this may be necessary for the fullest understanding of them. But he must also remember that his brief is to interpret religion sociologically; his values lie in a scientific discipline, and in consequence he must always maintain appropriate distance. It is sometimes objected by religious people that properly to understand a religion one must belong to it. Scholars in any of the disciplines that make religion their object of study cannot accept that. One does not need to be a medieval man to

---

[9] This methodological position may be supported in considerable measure from Max Weber's writings: see two discussions as translated into English, Max Weber, *The Methodology of the Social Sciences* (translated by Edward A. Shils and Henry A. Finch), Glencoe. Ill.: The Free Press, 1949; and Max Weber, *Basic Concepts in Sociology* (translated by H. P. Secher), London: Peter Owen, 1962.

study medieval society, nor a tribesman to understand a tribal group. Indeed, this objection to the sociological study of religion is an objection to the detached and objective approach of any academic discipline. We may, of course, concede the obvious fact that, at one level, the sociologist will never understand as much as does a believer of equal intelligence and perspicacity. At another level, however, since he sees from the outside, he may acquire a much sharper perspective about a religion and about the practices of its adherents than is possible for those who are committed and who can see only from the inside. Thus, at best, the sociologist should be able to add a whole dimension to the understanding of a religious movement which believers themselves could not obtain from their own perspective. In certain ways he will know less than they do; in other ways he will know more. Part of his way of knowing 'more' will of course come not only from his objectivity and detachment, but also from the fact that he has access, or should have access, to a wider body of information about other comparable religious movements. Comparison is a fundamental requirement of sociological method. From comparisons arise hypotheses of wider generality, and formulations that can transcend, in their abstraction, the circumstances of given cases. Without betraying the peculiarities and particularities of any given movement or any given cultural context, the sociologist should be able to gain some useful interpretative insight from an examination of comparable cases, and from the generalizations that his colleagues and teachers have already established with respect to them.

A number of problems arise from the distinctive stance adopted by the sociologist of religion, not all of which can be easily resolved. The basic problem for the investigator is implicit in his role: sympathy and detachment are not easily balanced. The demand for such balance may be a problem that is culturally more acute in the West than it is in the Far East. In the West, religious intolerance has been more pronounced, and for long periods of western history neither heretics nor agnostics were safe from religious persecution. Although such times have passed, there persists a residue of very high sensitivity on religious issues. Perhaps in some oriental cultures, in which more diffuse religious attitudes prevail, and in which different religious traditions co-exist, merge, or persist in symbiotic

relationship, the prospect of achieving sympathetic detachment, and of being credited with it by both believers and others,
is very much greater.

There are other problems which are often closely associated
with one another in practice, but which, for analytical purposes, we may treat separately. First, the application of scientific procedures to human phenomena presents difficulties.
The religious participants feel deeply about their faith. In some
respects it is for them not only the true interpretation of life, but
it is also inextricably part of life itself. Life is lived according to
the dictates of the truth as they see it, and, in consequence, their
religion becomes, for seriously committed people, what life is
about. Obviously, for the sociologist of religion, the religious
movement and its members are a subject matter that constitute
sociological phenomena. But no sociologist would succeed in
studying religion were he not to appreciate the profound
seriousness of religion to its adherents. He cannot therefore be
casually clinical in the way that, for example, medical men
sometimes appear to be casual in their clinical view of their
cases. Furthermore, the measure of his seriousness, in a sense his
dedication (even though it is dedication to his discipline—the
sociology of religion—and not to religion *per se*), is quickly
appraised by those whom he seeks as informants and
respondents.

Arising from this problem is the fact that scientific procedures
may easily appear profane in the context of religion. Usually,
people will much more readily discuss their leisure-time
pursuits—their work and industrial relations, their problems
arising from ecological and urban development, their political
opinions, and even their familial, kinship and sexual relationships and activities—than their religious dispositions and
beliefs. This very sensitivity of the area of enquiry—which is
perhaps more evident in some respects in the West—presents
the sociologist of religion with a delicate problem in the conduct
of his research. Not only must his attitude be much more
delicately attuned to the expectations of his respondents than is
the case in most other sociological research, but it is likely that
many of the methods of enquiry used by sociologists in other
fields are unavailable to him, or are usable only with great
circumspection. Above all, he must avoid the impression of
using methods that appear to trivialize, disparage, or relativize

the activities of his respondents. If he uses interview procedures in order to discover something about religious believers, he must check his instruments of research with respect to the language that he uses, the appropriateness of his questions, and the implications that his questions might appear to carry to others who are unacquainted with his purposes, or who do not accept them. In some respects, the interview is by far the best of the specifically sociological instruments available. It provides face-to-face contact between sociologist and respondent, and, providing the sociologist has some skill in inter-personal relationships, this opportunity in itself should allow him to dispel the doubts that his respondents may possibly entertain.

Interviews are, however, extremely time-consuming in themselves, and the yield from long periods of work is inevitably small. Sociology in general may be described as a 'distilling discipline' in the sense that it takes a mass of individual facts, and from them produces generalizations which are, inevitably, expressed in summary fashion. Large quantities of data are reduced, either by statistics or by theoretical formulations, into relatively concise propositions. In the case of the interview, the same distilling process is evident. Many interviews create a certain impression, and these impressions may be represented, perhaps in codified form, in very much shorter space and time than was involved in the eliciting of the information. There is a further problem involved, however: the yield from interviewing relative to the time expended is disappointingly small, and because, to be manageable, interviews are usually few in number, the statement of summarized interview findings may appear to be drawn from an insufficient basis of material and to be unduly subjective. Since his data are often so slender, and his interpretations so easily challenged, the sociologist of religion has to be unusually conscious of the need to maintain in the forefront of his mind the canons of objectivity.

Although, in the last analysis, this problem is not resolvable, alternative procedures in the sociology of religion are even more deficient. Questionnaires have limited value. They are useful for gathering gross data (age, sex, social position, occupation, education, etc.) but since religion is a very personal matter and always of great seriousness, to elicit information by impersonal means is to run the risk that one's enquiries may be interpreted as a type of profanation—a consequence that is much less likely when information is elicited by personal interview. Many data are themselves too complex to be elicited by questionnaire in any case, and the room for misunderstandings at both factual and intentional levels is considerable. Religion is a field in which quantification is particularly vulnerable to objection. It is not easy, except with the expression of simple and sometimes crude statements, to quantify the religious beliefs and dispositions of a particular population. It is quite impossible by these methods alone to interpret either religious belief or practice in its cultural and social meaning. Thus, methods that are normal in sociological enquiry in other areas of life and social organization have more limited application in the sociology of religion.

Limitations of the sociology of religion

Lying behind these problems with respect to specifically sociological methods are problems that relate to interpretation of the religious phenomena. For believers, it may well appear to be the case that no purely scientific representation can be adequate for their religion. In part, sociologists recognize this, and it is evident that sociological language is much more precise when dealing with systems that can be represented impersonally, such as bureaucracies, organizations, patterns of kinship, role systems, authority structures, and the like, than when seeking to communicate the distinctive qualities of religious movements and religious assemblies. Of course, the sociologists of religion are also interested in religious roles, authority, organization, and so on, but when all these elements have been explored and explained, there remains a variety of elements that are not so easily described in sociological language, and these are perhaps central features of religion in that they have to do with community and affectivity. A full appreciation of religious groups in the modern world depends not only upon an acquaintance with atmosphere, ethos, collective feeling, uplift, and inspiration, but on perceptive sensitivity to these things. 'Atmosphere', 'ethos', 'collective response' and so on, are not very sociological words, and it is not uncommon for sociologists when seeking to convey something of the ambience of a religious assembly or the expressive culture of a particular group to resort to what might be described as literary techniques of presentation, description which conveys by the use of emotive terms and impressions more than can be conveyed by the strictly neutral jargon and clinical language of the subject. Ultimately, the religiously-committed man may not accept these literary devices as capable of conveying anything of what he may regard as inexpressible elements of his religious culture. When he says, 'You must belong to it to understand it', or 'You must feel it to know what it is really about', the honest sociologist of religion knows that, at one level at least, these remarks are true.

Quite apart from the attempt to convey the distinctive character of a religious movement and its believers, there are problems that arise between sociologists and believers in the analysis by which sociologists seek to explain religious phenomena. To take only one important example, the sociologist will necessarily have in mind comparative cases when considering the development, general belief system, social composition, and social activities of any religious movement. He will wish to examine each movement in the light of the implicit understanding that is derived from the knowledge of other movements and other cultures. This is an implicit element of sociological procedure; comparison is vital to it. But there is a sense in which comparison must be odious to the committed adherents of any religion. Each religion is claimed as the most complete system and expression of ultimate truth, with warranted and necessary practices, and complete legitimation. This is more emphatically the case in the West, where religions have arisen in hostility to each other, and where exclusivism has been the norm. Adherents know, of course, that their own faith is not the only one that has claimed to possess the unique and universal truth, or at least to present a full expression of the truth which in other religions is understood at best partially; none the less, the idea that different movements might be examined in impartial comparison is not one that commends itself to religious believers. Here the divergent value orientations of the adherent and the sociologist become apparent, and the adherent is called upon to display a tolerance about sociological investigation which his own religious commitment may make difficult. There is no final solution to this problem for exclusivistic religions, even though in practice the point is not always pressed.

The intrinsic claims of a religion cannot be represented by the sociologist as direct first-order statements to his own public.

He must say, the members of religion X claim so-and-so. If he is careless in his formulation of their self-claim he may find himself in difficulty—and regarded as in some sense hostile to the movement he has been studying. Some years ago, I had to write a short *Encyclopaedia* article about Mormonism.[10] I said that the movement began in the United States in about 1830. That proposition is accepted by all non-Mormons, and might be tolerated even by Mormons, but to some very deeply-committed Mormons, it was a mis-statement: they claimed that their religion was at that time simply 're-founded' after its extinction for centuries. Clearly, if adherents are adamant that the movement's self-claims are the absolute truth, and beyond compromise, even for the benefit of a public which is uninstructed in it, the sociologist of religion will find himself in a position of unsurmountable difficulty.

The sociologist's terms of reference are to locate religion in its wider social context. His framework of explanation is bounded by the parameters of the social, by the social facts concerning the emergence of a particular set of religious ideas and practices, and the social composition of adherents. Clearly, part of the sociologist's work must be historical, and he may be interested in any of the usual historical issues—the provenance of particular ideas; the continuities or discontinuities in religious practice; the development of specific styles of religious organization; the impress of the secular society on the development of religion, and the effect of religion on the development of secular society; the origin and diffusion of a religious ethic; the extent to which religious commitment can be transferred generationally; the processes of conversion and persuasion; the relationship of magical to ethical precepts; the relation of religious movements to one another; the degree of localization of religious conceptions of the cosmos or the nomos; the process of religious unification and division, and so on. Even if full answers are obtained to all of these questions about the social dimensions of religion, it must be clear that the richness of religious phenomena is not exhausted. There are other levels of apprehension of religious information. There is the question of the mainsprings of commitment and its meaning to the believer.

Some of the issues that are raised in the sociology of religion border the territory claimed by psychology, but there are,

---

[10] This article appears in the current edition of the *Encyclopaedia Britannica*.

despite appearances, distinct differences of approach. The sociology of religion may proceed (although it has not always done so) according to the canons of methodological individualism.[11] However, even when it does so, it does not become an exercise in psychology. The concern with motivations in the sociology of religion is concern with 'typical' patterns of motivation as these might be located in terms of significant sociological variables—social class, education, sex, etc. It is not an attempt to provide an aetiology of motives. Thus one may move, as Max Weber moved with such consummate skill, from the discussion of the social ethic of a religious movement to a reconstruction of patterns of motivation among adherents. One can see a plausible psychological configuration which offers explanation of the individual's response to particular social pressures, but which does not *reduce* the social to distinctly or specifically psychological facts. Even where the discourse entails a hypothesization of individual motives, it is the social probability of these connections that matters, not the psychological determinants *per se*.

If the sociology of religion is not to be reduced to psychology, neither is it to be regarded as merely a branch of what is often called comparative religion, or *Religionswissenschaft*, even though comparison is very much part of its method. A sociologist's approach differs from what I take to be that of comparative religionists because the sociologist has ultimate commitment to explain religion by reference to broad theoretical propositions about society.[12] Religion is taken as a social fact, and the sociologist is not concerned merely to describe or expound the beliefs, practices, artefacts, doctrines, and organization of religion, intrinsically interesting as they may be. He seeks to find, beneath the overlay of specific cultural style and content, social structural principles. Sociology as we have said, is a *distilling* discipline—and this not only with reference to the reduction of large bodies of detailed facts by analytical procedures, but also in the reduction of diverse cultural contents

---

[11] For discussion of methodological individualism, see Sir Karl Popper, *The Open Society and its Enemies*, London: Routledge, 1945; and idem, *The Poverty of Historicism*, London: Routledge, 1957; see the useful discussion in Steven Lukes, *Individualism*, Oxford: Blackwell, 1973, especially pp. 110–22.

[12] I take as a representative recent example of the discipline of *Religionswissenschaft*, the account of Jacques Waardenburg, '*Religionswissenschaft* New Style: Some Thoughts and Afterthoughts', *Annual Review of the Social Sciences of Religion*, 2, 1978, pp. 189–220.

to theoretical statements which are set out in relatively abstract terms, and which set out fundamental relationships. Clearly, the lengths to which this procedure is taken must differ with the explanatory purpose being pursued, and I for my part should not wish to advocate abstract theory merely for its own sake. None the less, the thrust of the discipline is clear: comparison is a method and not an object for the sociology of religion.

We may mark a similar distinction between the sociologist and the phenomenologist. The phenomenologist appears to regard facts as a good in their own right, seeking to set out faithfully—and with an objectivity to which the sociologist also aspires—the details of specific religious phenomena. Many of these details are, of necessity, social in character, and to this extent part of the work of these two types of investigator may overlap. But as a sociologist sees it, the phenomenologist may sometimes be in danger of supposing that the facts 'speak for themselves'. He may forget that practices and beliefs carry implicit meanings which are culturally specific, and these meanings are an order of data which the sociologist seeks to explore. The unwillingness of the phenomenologist to structure his data and to select his material contrasts with the sociologist's insistence that, by any standards, selectivity occurs in every academic and scientific enquiry, and since it must occur, then it had better be undertaken with deliberate and conscious intent, and according to principles that are themselves open to critical evaluation and re-evaluation. The sociologist makes conscious decisions about the relevance of particular items of fact, and indeed about whole orders of factual information; he is aware that he must make judgements of value-relevance. He structures his information, aware that to do so is to jeopardize the canons of objectivity that he jealously seeks to preserve. His safeguards in this operation lie essentially in his self-consciousness about the process in which he is engaged, in his sustained self-criticism about his assumptions and methods and in his awareness that analysis must vary according to his pre-conceived ideas about the research. Thus it is that sociologists often spend a great deal of time elaborating their methodological procedures, to the point, at times, of becoming unduly obsessive about them. The point, however, is clear: since facts have to be selected, better that such selection be conscious and deliberate and subject to criticism. Finally, the sociologist must also recognize that no exercise in sociological analysis is to be regarded as in any sense definitive; the assumptions, procedures, and methods employed in any given investigation may all be amended or abandoned in favour of better ones in a subsequent research enquiry. In this way the balance might be struck between the commitment to scientific objectivity and the need to avoid crude positivism. Because his data are not only phenomenological fact, but include the values of those who, as a first-order experience, deal with these facts, the sociologist needs to see his role as implicitly and unavoidably interpretative. Recognizing his own interpretative role, he seeks also to account for the interpretations that are made by the participants in all social—and all religious—life.

Clearly, sociology is not a form of theological apologetics, even though the development of what was sometimes called sociology occurred among some Christian clergy. Given that sociology developed originally in the context of Christian culture, it would be surprising had this not been the case. The radical anti-theological stance of early sociology was disregarded by these clerics, of course, and what emerged, particularly in France and Belgium, under the label of *sociologie religieuse*, was a type of sociography, pursued with specific problems of pastoral theology in mind.[13] These religiously-committed sociologists sought principally to trace the patterns of Christian influence in society, in relation, for example, to industrialization, and to discover the connections between geographic patterns of religious practice and specific local historical traditions. These studies fall short of a fully-fledged sociology of religion. They do so because their perspectives are usually limited to one religious confession; because they lack a sociological basis of explanatory theory; and because they often have recourse to normative propositions both in discussing historical facts and in their advocacy of church policies and programmes. Analysis was started from a point at which Christianity was assumed to be the normal and the incontestable commitment to the discipline. Sociological variables were deployed and statistical findings produced, but there was in this tradition an unwillingness to ask the type of theoretical

---

[13] The doyen of this school was Gabriel Le Bras. For a recent example of its work, see F. Boulard, *An Introduction to Religious Sociology* (translated by Michael Jackson), London: Darton, Longman, and Todd, 1960.

questions that have appropriately been asked by sociologists of religion—namely, questions about the underlying functions of religious adherence; the differential appeal of religion according to the specifics of particular classes or social groups; and the substitutability of one set of religious beliefs for another, or of secular beliefs and activities for religious ideas and practices. Most practitioners of *sociologie religieuse* were clerics of the Roman Church, but as, in recent decades, the posture of that church has changed, so the distinctiveness of their approach has diminished; *sociologie religieuse* is today a disappearing designation.

One may refer to two signs of the times in this matter. First, some of the institutes of socio-religious research which the churches in Europe (both Catholic and Protestant) supported in the late 1950s and 60s, have now ceased to function. Second, the principal international organization of sociologists of religion, *Conférence internationale de sociologie religieuse*, which, as its name suggests, was founded by Catholic priests who wished to acquire a better understanding of the social influences that operated on their religion, and which their religion exercised in society, has recently decided to change its name to the *Conférence internationale de sociologie des religions*. The change is in fact belated in that the CISR has, since the late 1960s, been committed to a thoroughly scientific and academic approach, embracing the highest standards of neutral and objective scholarship. The desire of the leading members to divest the organization from its earlier, specifically Catholic, associations became evident, in 1971, in its election of a new President, who was neither a Catholic nor even a Christian.

The scientific orientation of the sociology of religion is deliberate. The steady consolidation of this position among those who investigate religion in its social implications has created a sense of distinction between this explicitly professional commitment and the work of religiously-committed commentators which is necessarily regarded as amateur. This is not to say that a sociologist of religion cannot be *personally* a religiously-committed man; clearly that is a possibility. But in his sociological work he must adopt the professional stance of the detached, neutral, and objective investigator; and this we may take as a necessary qualification.

Yet the discipline itself still struggles with an inheritance of cultural bias that has not been entirely expunged—and the last traces of which may, in the nature of things—remain ineradicable. Precisely because the professional stance is now so clearly articulated, it becomes all the more important for sociologists to recognize the existence of these cultural and religiously-inspired predispositions. We have noted that sociology developed as a discipline in the context of Christian culture. Thus, the early conceptions of religion that sociologists entertained were heavily suffused with the ideas, ethos, and atmosphere of Christianity. Nor was this merely a matter of the external and superficial forms of worship and symbols. It very much affected the ideas that sociologists developed concerning the social functions of religion; that extent of penetration of religious consciousness into social life; and the relationship of religion and morality. Some of the basic categories of analysis were all too evidently drawn from Christian theological concepts, such as the distinction between the sacred and the profane; this-worldly and other-wordly; clergy and laity; and orthodoxy and heresy. Other categories, such as particularism and universalism, may have a less tainted provenance, but in their application to the religious field, it was perhaps too easy for sociologists to assume that the western case—that is the Christian case—provided the paradigm by which all other cases might be analysed.

The sociology of religion is still in some degree in captivity to its concepts—concepts of Christian provenance. Any external critic must, however, recognize two things: that this is a captivity and not a voluntary commitment; and that at least some sociologists are aware of it. To break completely free may not be possible, since the sociologist needs concepts that 'make sense' of new cases and alien instances, and these are necessarily concepts understood within his own fraternity and derived from the cultural context in which that fraternity learned its terms of discourse. He cannot be bound by the concepts, explicit or implicit, of the culture or the religion that he studies, even though he must, perforce, be thoroughly acquainted with them. His task is, after all, to 'translate' these into the language of his discipline, even though that language, too, is culturally conditioned. Of course, he must, as we have said, first understand, both rationally and empathically, the meanings and purposes, the consciousness and atmosphere, the symbolism and organization of those whose activities he studies. But he cannot leave his task there. He must transmit what he has learned in a language understood by the public which sponsors his work, or which at least 'receives' it—and that particular public is, first and foremost, his academic colleagues, those within his own profession. If the language of that public is less than hermetically sealed—and this is in the nature of such languages—then he must take such measures as he can to sterilize his terms as he goes along, thereby reducing the prospect of cultural infection of his material. We do not live in a world of pure concepts, and even the frictionless pistons and perfect lubricants of thermodynamics are no more than convenient fictions. In us the use of ideal-type constructs, sociologists (including the sociologists of religion) adopt similar devices, even though the sterilization of sociological concepts is more difficult and more delicate. The sociologist's defence, however, in this matter, as in so many others that touch fundamentally on the notion of the enterprise in which he is engaged, is continued awareness of the difficulties inherent in his own activities and his own analysis. This is implied in his professionalism. On the one hand he must interpret his material to his professional colleagues, and on the other he must maintain faith with those whose religious concerns have been the object of his enquiry. The balance of these two preoccupations clearly varies, both between pieces of work, and, whenever field-work is involved, within the same particular piece of research. If I give the last word to the problem of field-work, that perhaps reflects something of the balance of my own contemporary concerns.

For his religious public, the professional sociologist of religion is something of a curiosity. Here is a man seen to be deeply interested in religion and (one may hope) seen to be widely informed about it. And yet he is not, and quite deliberately not, a religiously-committed man—at least, whilst practising his sociology. The religious people with whom he works know that his values are not their values. And yet he clearly knows a great deal about the religion he is studying. Sometimes respondents say, as they have said to me, 'You know a lot about us; you know about the truth: why do you not join us?'. It is a difficult—a fundamental—question; but it is an understandable question and a perfectly proper question. The sociologist cannot say, 'I know what you think is the truth, but I do not accept it'. Indeed, it would be professionally wrong to discuss what one accepted or rejected as 'the truth'. The respondents know that one is not committed to their perspective. They ask because they have a genuine concern for another human being—and if they are concerned, this is an indication that they perceive the sympathy which a sociologist of religion must feel for his respondents. To be asked is to be paid a compliment. But it is also a dilemma. The best answer that I can give to such a question is to say, as I have said on occasions, 'You must regard me as a photographer. Since I am taking pictures of what I find, I cannot be in the picture myself.' It is not a perfect reply, and it does not solve the serious implications of the question, but it maintains the investigator's detachment and the integrity of the professional nature of his commitment; it sustains the necessary sympathetic relationship of investigator and respondent; and it provides some analogous justification for the meeting point of their different set of values.

2

The Functions of Religion in Contemporary Society

Salvation: a manifest concern

The explicit and manifest function of religion is to offer men the prospect of salvation and to provide them with appropriate guidance for its attainment. Obviously, just what is taken to constitute salvation differs from one culture and one religion to another. Man has conceived of salvation in a wide variety of ways. Sometimes it has been culturally phrased as triumph over death, either through the migration to a higher plane of a man's soul or spirit, or by the miraculous resurrection of the body at some future time. Such have been the elements that Christianity inherited from its Greek and Hebrew predecessors. In other cultures, death is regarded as not so traumatic an event, and salvation is sought rather from the evil prevalent in earthly life. In Hinduism, the fulfilment of the obligations of caste dharma is believed to ensure the eventual progression of the individual through many reincarnations to a higher condition of life, until he experiences unity with the supreme deity.[1] In Theravada Buddhism, the ultimate experience of salvation is thought to lie in the attainment of nirvana and the cessation of all desire, whilst in Buddhism of the northern tradition, the emphasis is very much more on the attainment of a high state of grace from which to reach out and offer help to others who are seeking salvation in this world.[2] In less-developed religions, salvation

[1] For a recent lucid account of Hinduism, see Louis Dumont, *Homo Hierarchicus*, London: Weidenfeld and Nicolson, 1970; a less sociological account is provided in Sir Charles Eliot, *Hinduism and Buddhism: An Historical Sketch*, London: Routledge 1921, 3 vols.

[2] On Buddhism, the following short introductions may be found useful: Edward Conze (ed.), *Buddhist Scriptures*, Harmondsworth: Penguin, 1959; idem, *Buddhism: Its Essence and Development*, London: Faber, 1951; Walpola Rahula, *What the Buddha Taught*, New York: Grove Press, 1959; Hans Wolfgang Schumann, *Buddhism: An Outline of its Teaching and Schools*, London: Rider, 1973; Arthur F. Wright, *Buddhism in Chinese History*, Stanford: Stanford University Press, 1959.

may in practice be very much more narrowly conceived, perhaps simply as the curing of disease, or the elimination of witchcraft, or even as the overcoming of one particular sorcerer's curse.

The extent to which salvation is conceptualized as particular and individual, or as communal and local, or as national and societal, also varies in different cultures, and sometimes even within one culture. The development of a more elevated conception of salvation—such, for example, as the Christian idea of life-after-death, or in the life-enhancing teaching of bodhisattva in Mahayana Buddhism—does not at once eradicate all more proximate, personal, or local ideas of salvation. Indeed, the elimination of local and particularistic notions of salvation has by no means always been regarded as essential for the dissemination of a more encompassing, universalistic, and rationalized soteriology.[3] Whilst it is true that the higher religions have in general reduced the operation of local magic, and have sought a hermeneutic of a wide-ranging and more abstract kind, even such a vigorously exclusivist and anti-magical religion as Christianity absorbed less-developed conceptions of salvation, and treated them virtually as auxiliary benefits arising from faith. Thus, in the Christian case, the healing of disease, although intermittently relegated or ignored, has been a recurrent expectation among the devout, and it is arguable that only through the belief in such healings did Christian teaching succeed in making its initial impact. In general, Christians are taught not to expect direct answers to prayer, and not to seek very specific benefits from their relations with their god, but, from its beginnings, people have claimed to be healed by faith, and, well within the bounds of orthodox belief and practice, there continue to be special facilities, places, and pilgrimages which, and individuals who, concentrate on the Christian healing of the body.[4]

We may regard such demands for performance as one aspect of the salvation that religions promise, and even in advanced and intellectualized religious systems which embrace a more

[3] For an excellent study of the elimination of magic by Christianity, see Keith Thomas, *Religion and the Decline of Magic*, London: Weidenfeld and Nicolson, 1971; see also Bryan R. Wilson, *Magic and the Millennium: Religious Movements of Protest among Tribal and Third-World Peoples*, London: Heinemann, 1973, pp. 105ff.

[4] For a discussion of this issue, see James N. Lapsley, *Salvation and Health*, Philadelphia: Westminster Press, 1972.

elevated conception of salvation as a spiritual prospect, this concern with cure is not displaced. One feature of these more elevated and theologically better-rationalized soteriological schemes is that they remove the test of salvation from the empirical sphere. Reincarnation, Nirvana, the life of the soul, and the kingdom of God, are what may be termed *spiritual* conceptions of salvation. They have in common the inapplicability of empirical proofs. The goals are themselves metaphysical, and the means to their attainment are insusceptible of rational justification or pragmatic test. In this they differ from what we may refer to as *particularistic* conceptions of salvation, in which specific help is sought—cures; protection; temporal well-being. By promoting spiritual conceptions of salvation, to which empirical proofs are irrelevant, and by denying the ultimate warranty of such proofs even in those instances in which material benefits are sought, the higher religions assert their difference from the purely magical and the local.

Salvation, in all the higher religions, is to be attained (or affirmed) by ethical action, and in the nature of ethical concerns the balance between effort and reward is not finely calculated, it is often emphasized that it must not be calculated at all ('Take no thought for your life, what ye shall eat, or what ye shall drink' is the way in which Jesus Christ put it). Precise calculation would contravene the spirit of elevated conceptions of salvation; being 'saved' is manifested by transcending any tight or narrow concern for just deserts, recompense, or anything that may be called 'meanness of spirit'. It is only the quasi-magical that operates according to rules of specified 'in-put' and calculated return. Yet, even though we may draw this clear line between elevated and local conceptions of salvation, in practice all religions embrace both. Vague rewards are often supplemented by actual empirical benefits, but no high religion rests its case on rewards alone. Nor do such religions—even though material blessings be accepted as aids to faith—consider that they should be taken as final proofs. Yet the founders of the great religions, and the prophets and saints of other traditions, wrought their miracles as testimonies of the truth of their claims. They did not reject lesser evidence of the greater salvation which, in its totality, was not provable. The faith that made men whole was in its healing performance, an earnest of what would eventually be achieved. The first concern, however, was to be spiritual salvation. Thus, in Christianity, men were first and foremost to seek 'the kingdom of God'; thereafter it was promised that 'all these other things will be added unto you'. The release that was to be attained in nirvana did not prevent the Gotama Buddha canvassing his message by reference to the immediate and temporal benefits that might accrue to the faithful. The Buddha told householders how they might by virtue acquire wealth, reputation, confidence, and self-possession, experience death without anxiety, and the prospect of being reborn in a happy state in heaven—all without prejudice, apparently, to the ideal of attaining nirvana. So it is that the prayers and the meditation of the faithful everywhere seek well-being *now* as well as benefit hereafter. These very diverse items are all incorporated in what, in social practice and as social aspiration, may be said to constitute salvation.

The tendency of the higher religions is to embrace all mankind as the constituency for salvation. This universalism should not obscure the fact that what is offered is also offered specifically to individuals. The great religions emphasize the individual's own responsibility for seeking salvation, and in the Judaeo-Christian-Muslim traditions and that of Buddhism it is the individual who is specifically addressed. Salvation is universally available but each individual must make some personal effort or choice. Yet it must also be clear that no individual conceives of himself attaining salvation in isolation. What he conceives as salvation is necessarily influenced by his social experience of just what constitutes conditions of well-being. A man's idea of well-being is itself socially conditioned; it is something that he has learned in his own immediate local community. In the great religions those seeking salvation are increasingly envisaged as being a body of believers who have chosen to follow a path, and who become a putative community of the faithful recognizably seeking salvation in their own eyes and in the eyes of other men. Yet it is, for most individuals, in the life of the actual community in which they live that a state of greater blessing is conceived. The living community becomes the model of a context in which spiritual salvation will be experienced. Even if there is no ultimate doctrinal legitimation for such a belief, and even if all that has been said, for example, about the Kingdom of Heaven, or nirvana, cannot be reconciled with these communally-derived notions, there can, none the less, be no doubt about the communal nature of what we might call the operative conceptions of salvation. In modern urban society, the local community is no longer a natural 'living group' bound by ties of kin, neighbourhood, and a shared past. In the West, the religious expression of such so-called 'communities' (neighbourhoods might be a better word) is often defunct or operates only perfunctorily. Religious fellowships continue, of course, but they are no longer coterminous with local communities. Rather they are drawn from wider areas into what becomes quite literally (and not in the specific Protestant sense of the term) a 'gathered' community of committed believers—a church membership or a sectarian congregation. But, even in this circumstance, it is often the persisting traditional idea of the 'natural' community which serves as a model for the assumption and the aspirations of men concerning the conditions of salvation. Men discover their purposes and live out their obligations in a network of social relationships, and they necessarily envisage the condition of salvation as something that might be attained by, or which is even contained within, the ideal community life. Until very recently men had experienced almost all of their purposes and obligations in the local community. The extension of salvation to embrace all mankind came with the great religions, but it has remained beyond the immediate ken of the vast majority of men. It remains more of a religious ideology than of an immediate expectation, since no religion embraces more than a fragment of this constituency.

From a sociological point of view, what all these various applications of the idea of salvation have in common is that what they all proffer is present reassurance. Whatever form cultural, local, or personal anxieties may take, religion offers to still these anxieties by recourse to reassuring beliefs, practices, or facilities. The sacred literature of the great religions recounts episodes of human anxiety and anguish, and the ways in which such experience may be assuaged. All religions provide a vocabulary of sufferings, whether these are personal, communal, societal, or even universal in kind, and they provide, no less, a repertoire of methods for their relief. But it has been at local level that men have mostly looked for evidences of salvation. As long as religion appeared effective in the affairs of men—and it did so over man's long history of living in local communities (in contradistinction to living in impersonal contexts in mass society)—it offered personal or local immediate reassurance. Psychological reassurance is an element common to all religions, despite the diversity of the issues that give rise to anxiety among men. Sometimes this reassurance is expressed as hope. Whatever other concerns particular religions may articulate, the provision of this reassurance in one or several of the forms we have discussed so far, is the manifest function that religions have in common.

The latent functions of religion

I have mentioned first this manifest function of religion, because, in approaching social organization from the positivistic and rationalistic perspective implicit in science, sociologists have been very much more disposed to discuss religion in terms of its latent functions—the functions that arise unseen or unintended by men in the practice of their religion.[5] Sociologists asked why people believed particular myths for which specific empirical evidence was lacking; or why people engaged in practices the reasons for which were not immediately obvious; or why men accepted a variety of superempirical goals, the means of attaining which were not capable of any specific pragmatic test. They answered these questions not in the same terms as the believers, but by reference to functions which sociologists came to believe that religion subserved. These functions were latent in the sense that believers did not themselves know of them; for them religion was an obligation, a necessity, the 'given' means of coping with the world. Their own reasons for practising were embedded in values and sentiments that were by no means easily analysed and about which they were, in most cases, neither self-conscious not intellectually curious. The sociologist, however, revealed relationships that transcended the understanding of believers about their own society and its operation. They uncovered evidence to show just what vital support men gave to their social organization by participating in religion.

The functionalist theory of religion was first propounded by Emile Durkheim with respect to the social organization of

[5] The distinction is elaborated by Robert K. Merton, *Social Theory and Social Structure*, Glencoe, Ill.: The Free Press, revd. edn. 1957, pp. 20–84.

aboriginal tribes in Australia.[6] Durkheim maintained that religious activity allowed these tribes to take cognizance of themselves as collectivities, to symbolize their social order, and, in the representation of a totemic animal, to gain an objective sense of their own society. One of the functions of religion for such a people was that their myths and rituals permitted them to entertain collective sentiments and express a sense of social unity. Religion, then, functioned to maintain social cohesion. When people were brought together for solemn acts—acts too awful to contemplate in any other context than in the presence of the whole community—so they unwittingly gained a renewed and serious sense of themselves and of the legitimacy of their social organization. They ascribed both the sense of well-being and its substance to their deity.

What Durkheim maintained for Australian tribes subsequently became the more general anthropological wisdom of the functionalist school. Subsequently, sociologists applied the same type of functionalist analysis to advanced societies. What these functionalists postulated was a close relationship between social structure and function. They maintained that religion subserved a variety of functions in society, but that these functions were latent rather than explicit. Religion provided occasions of reunion, the reassertion of social solidarity, and so sustained social cohesion, and it solemnized the social order, so providing a basis for what sociologists used to call social control. That is to say, they saw religion as prescribing moral norms, which were enjoined on the people as requirements of a higher supernatural order. Sometimes—and the Judaeo-Christian tradition provided a good example of this—there were specific religiously-described sanctions of behaviour. Good behaviour was the way to win merit in the economy of the divine order, while bad deeds would incur punishments that would be visited on wrong-doers, perhaps in this world, but certainly in the life to come. Commitment to, or defection from, caste dharma in Hinduism clearly attracted comparable consequences in future reincarnations.

Religions usually account for (or allow men to discount, as in Theravada Buddhism) the physical universe. They offer, at any rate, an explanation of physical phenomena even if they do not

[6] See Emile Durkheim, *The Elementary Forms of the Religious Life* (1915) (translated by J. W. Swain), Glencoe: Ill.: The Free Press, 1954.

(as so strongly in the Judaeo-Christian case) provide a creation myth. More significantly, at the more immediate level of the social, religion functioned to legitimize the purposes and procedures of society itself. It sustained men in their commitments; reinforced their resolve in struggle; justified their wars; explained misfortunes; provided a final court of appeal for disputes; sanctified specific relationships and courses of action; and prescribed a variety of reassuring techniques with which men could equip themselves psychologically, whether in undertaking their day-to-day tasks or in embarking upon a once-in-a-lifetime enterprise.

Attention has recently been paid to the function of religion in conferring identity on individuals and groups, or in reinforcing the sense of identity derived from other associations or affiliations.[7] Religion answered the question, 'Who am I?' for individuals, and 'Who are we?' for groups. Religious answers to these questions attain the highest and most general level at which an answer can be provided; they locate the individual or the group in cosmic space and in an eternal order. Religion responds to these questions with finality and totality. Acceptance of its answers implies, at least in more advanced religions, the acceptance of a metaphysical scheme of things within which the specific answer acquires its meaning.

Finally, religion has functioned as an agency for emotional expression and regulation. This function is analytically distinguishable from that of social control, but, in practice, control of the emotions is a vital part of social control, since mass emotions in particular may quickly be disruptive of stable social order. In religious acts and occasions, there is the opportunity for the expression of emotion, but by implication the provision of specific contexts and occasions that facilitate emotional expression is also, implicitly, a way of regulating that expression. Ritual in particular is an agency for the regulation, as well as for the facilitation, of the expression of emotion: to plagiarize an English poet, one might say that ritual is emotion recollected in tranquillity. Religious ritual stimulates, often in a relatively gentle way, certain types of emotional expression. Response is elicited, expression is encouraged, and the means of the assuagement of emotions is then provided. We may say that

---

[7] See Hans Mol, *Identity and the Sacred: A Sketch for a New Social-Scientific Theory of Religion*, Oxford: Blackwell, 1976.

ritual manages the emotions: it provides the occasion and the means for their decorous and controlled expression. Clearly, men's emotional needs may arise in the conduct of their individual daily lives, in coping with the untoward, or in dealing with puzzling and distressing contingencies; in religion these emotions are elevated, solemnized, rekindled, and assuaged in symbolic action. The religious group may itself engender emotional commitment from those who participate, and its own success may in part depend on its capacity to summon such response. Such a group may itself become the focus of intense emotional concern for its members, and religious exercises necessarily include occasions for the celebration of the existence of the group, and the dedication of men to its continuance and its goals.

These, then, are what sociologists have seen as the latent functions of religion, and there is no doubt that they have found this concept extremely attractive. Many sociologists held rationalistic assumptions and they were, consequently, exercised by the persistence of what they regarded as the irrational.[8] How were they to explain these religious activities that were, from a rational point of view, meaningless and arbitrary, undertaken in the service of myths and ideas that could, empirically, be shown to be either unprovable or patently false? Latent functional analysis supplied the answers: religion persisted, not because its explicit orientations were convincing, but because in respects that were not at all explicit, it served society in these various ways.

The appeal of this type of theorizing is obvious: it allowed the sociologist to explain the resilience of the non-rational, which to men adopting rationalistic perspectives was a difficult conundrum. And of course, this type of explanation had the additional gratification that sociologists generally have derived from debunking. Religion was, above all other social institutions, most amenable to this mode of explanation. In almost all other pursuits, what men did might be explained directly and in accordance with their own apprehensions of their activities. Economic concerns generally, and political and social activities increasingly, succumbed to analysis that followed rational and

<hr />

[8] Kingsley Davis took this position quite explicitly; see K. Davis, *Human Society*, New York: Macmillan, 1948, where he writes, 'Religious beliefs are certainly not true in any scientific sense, but their social function does not depend on their being true', p. 535

empirical principles. Science and technology were, of course, the epitome of rational organization, and manifest functions and explicit purposes were the obvious departure point for any sociological analysis of these institutions. And this was increasingly true for law and education. The family and its attendant institutions presented a more difficult case, being an accommodation of the socially functional and the biologically given; but, at least here, what could not be satisfactorily explained on rational premises could be attributed to deeper-laid biological demands. In any case, the family was an institution that, in its inherent nature, escaped central organization. It accommodated the distributive (rather than the collective) needs of a population, and so was less susceptible to rational principle. But religion—seemingly so non-sensical—presented the real occasion for latent functional analysis, by which sociologists sought to reveal the deeper levels at which the hidden mainsprings of religious vitality operated. Sociologists generally and unquestioningly supposed that latent functional analysis offered stronger explanations for the persistence of religion than did the invocation of manifest and explicit purposes—the provision of salvation—which was the type of explanation that might be offered by the religiously-committed themselves.

Yet, if we examine the place of religion in contemporary society, we may question whether these latent functions continue to be of such importance. Perhaps, in some respects, they were discovered and proclaimed on evidence that was too much drawn from tribal peoples and historical Christianity. Many of these latent functions of religion appear to have been taken over by other agencies, and, whatever religion now supplies to its votaries, or to society at large, in general it does not fulfil the latent functions that sociological theory has in the past generally ascribed to it. Briefly, we may review the evidence.

Latent functions in advanced societies
Contemporary society is increasingly pluralist in its cultural manifestations, including religion. In the West, this arises in part from the various waves of migration. Such migrations were, indeed, the very making of the north American states, but migration has increasingly affected Britain and continental

European countries, and parts of central and south America. Such migrations create new ethnic and religious diversity within the confines of nation-state societies. Even where migration has not occurred there has been a process of religious diffusion, so that there are Christian or Muslim minorities in many Asian countries, and there are numerous, different groups within each of these minorities. Within dominant religious traditions, it is the rule rather than the exception that there are different denominations or sects; such has been the case within Christianity, in Buddhism, and in the various schools of Hinduism. These movements may simply disregard each other, but more often there is at least distrust, and sometimes rivalry, competition, or thinly-veiled mutual hostility. Not unusually, these religious groups espouse divergent moral norms, and even if the ultimate values to which they are committed might, in abstract terms, be stated in similar formulations, none the less, their operative schemes of morality may differ significantly, and this may be enough to create competition and conflict among them. Given such diversity, can it any longer be suggested that religion functions to sustain social cohesion?

The extent to which religions have legitimated social order by the canvas of legal, moral, or customary norms has varied. But even in the Judaeo-Christian tradition, in which moral order has been heavily underwritten by religious interdictions and restraints, it can scarcely be said, in the secular societies of the West, that control of behaviour today depends on religious sanctions. At one time, the promise of a heavenly after-life for those who behaved well, and punishment and torment in hell for those who transgressed the moral law, were strong psychic reinforcements of proper social comportment.[9] They covered issues and attitudes that were not always covered by the law itself, and Christian priests interpreted their mission as, at least in part, to ensure as fully as they could that men would not commit crimes or cause social disruption. The relative natural law, as Christian teaching expounded it, was that since man was a fallen and sinful creature, there could be no perfect justice in this world. In that circumstance, the Church sought to urge

---

[9] Successive public opinion polls in Britain show a steady trend in the diminution of the proportion of people who believe in hell. The process has been long drawn out, however. For a study of the early evidences, see D. P. Walker, *The Decline of Hell: Seventeenth Century Discussions of Eternal Torment*, London: Routledge, 1964.

upon the rich and powerful their duties to the poor, and to persuade them to be merciful as a disposition pleasing to God, and as a source of better prospects in the life after death. On the other hand, the poor were exhorted to be content with their lot, to behave with respect and obedience to their social superiors, in the strong faith that such good behaviour in this world would ensure them better prospects in the life hereafter. Nowadays, however, the law has become more encompassing with respect to all overt acts likely to disturb social relations, while purely personal moral matters have tended to drop out of account. The law has ceased in large part to attempt to enforce morals upon the public. A wide variety of acts, particularly sexual acts, which were once matters for the law, have now ceased to be of concern to the public authorities, and this change has occurred in several western countries. On the other hand, a great many issues that are often little more than technical matters have become subject to legal control. Thus, religion has come to have less place in reinforcing social control, and many of the issues on which religious teaching has pronounced, have ceased to be regarded as matters for social regulation.

The change from moral to technical preoccupations of the law has led to the process of the socialization of children being regarded in an entirely different way from that in which it was traditionally seen: today parents no longer attempt to provide children with a religiously supported framework of attitudes and orientations from which in later life to judge moral matters. Religion is much less invoked in the inculcation of moral attitudes. It may indeed be hypothesized that, as the law becomes increasingly concerned with technical matters, so a much more specific calculus of right and wrong becomes the basis for a 'moral' education, from which diffuse goodwill and disinterested commitment, which the old religiously-inspired codes sustained, is being increasingly eroded.

In no advanced society does it today fall to religion to provide interpretations of the physical universe. The creation myths, which some religions included as part of their scheme of things, are widely discredited.[10] Men no longer look to religion for

[10] There are periodic demands in the mid-west and southern states of the United States for biblical theories of creation to be taught in state schools, but this pious biblicism appears to have no impact whatsoever on the assumptions on which the social system operates, and is manifestly contrary to all the procedures of contemporary scientific research.

information about the natural and physical order, even if they continue to accept these myths as allegories with symbolic meaning and poetic and aesthetic appeal. The natural sciences are now undisputed in their discoveries about the natural order, and many men accept the best that science can offer by way of explanation. Certainly the social system as such does not depend on religious interpretations of natural forces. Similarly, in advanced countries wars, political parties, the conduct of disputes, and entrepreneurial activity are today rarely supported by religious legitimations, and where religion provides symbolic identity for what amount to 'tribal' or ethnic groups, it does so usually without the sanctification of the religious authorities—as in Northern Ireland. Governments regulate their decisions by quite different points of reference; when politicians seek auguries they turn, not to the religious functionaries to provide prognostications or to interpret the will of God, but to public opinion polls. Some businessmen may still commit to prayer their concern for the well-being of their enterprises, but this could be so only for small businesses in private hands, which constitute a diminishing proportion of the volume of trade. The boards of directors of large impersonally organized corporations find a place on their agenda for market research, but one may safely speculate that none of them accord time to the discussion of the religious implications of business activity.

Even if we turn to the matter of identity, we see that although individuals and groups may seek reinforcement of their self-conceptions from religious sources, modern nation states do not rely on whatever religious legitimations may be written in their constitutions. Indeed, most modern state societies are essentially secular in conception. Many older states have abrogated the laws that gave a privileged place to one particular religion, while a significant number of newer states are founded not only on secular, but even on explicitly atheistic, philosophies. Only in states that have developed with great rapidity into the contemporary technical epoch have traditional religious dispositions persisted. These two divergent and often directly opposed orientations to the world give rise to social and political tension and to the possibility of anti-modern revolutionary movements. Wherever technical advance has occurred in only limited areas of economic and society, and without the widespread diffusion of new pragmatic and instrumental dispositions and value-orientations, such tensions must arise. Even in those thoroughly modernized societies in which there have evolved value-systems that support the technical, economic order, it is not to religious sources that we can point as the basis of value-consensus. Indeed, in such countries there is often considerable religious diversity, and if religion were really the continuing source of the values by which men ordered their affairs these religiously pluralist societies would also be marked by intense religious conflict. It is because religion receives so much less attention as a source of values that conflict does not occur. Clearly, then, religion is no longer the source of value-consensus in these societies.

With respect to the expression and regulation of the emotions, there are today vigorous competing agencies which seek to manipulate emotional life. Many of these agencies, such as television, films, and pop music, have at their disposal channels of communication which are technically more advanced and more effective than those that are available even to the most powerful religious groups. Their appeal is all the greater, perhaps, because emotional experience, in these contexts, is entirely divorced from moral exhortation and even from civic or social commitment. It need not even be presented—as was the case when emotion was summoned by religion—as justified or righteous. Emotion is rarely mobilized for moral causes by these modern agencies (except, perhaps, when morality can be politicized and turned into a matter of public moral outrage about some invasion of so-called natural justice). Generally, the emotions can be indulged hedonistically; sentiments are aroused for no better reason than personal gratification, whereas under the auspices of religion even if such gratification were attained it was always cloaked under the warrant of serious obligation. Emotional control is now left to each individual acting autonomously on the laissez-faire assumption that, without much overt cultural consensus on such issues, and with less and less direct effort in the education of the emotions, somehow every individual will strike a balance that will be socially acceptable. (What is socially acceptable itself becomes a shifting standard, of course). The increased openness of gambling, the manipulation of men's will to gain without effort, the increasingly open supply of, and the open demand for, pornography, are all indications of the efficient exploitation of men's emotions. In catering to the new open style of the emotional life, these agencies do not address men at the times of their most profound emotional need, during the traumas of life, but they do undertake extensive emotional manipulation and control over large sections of contemporary society, often trivializing emotional experience. They may even create a climate in which it ceases to be possible to rekindle the old religiously-induced emotional dispositions when emotion was harnessed in the service of morality. With such powerful competition, can it be maintained that regulation of the emotions is still today a latent function of religion that has much social significance?

If the foregoing analysis is at all correct, it would appear that the latent functions of religion, as sociologists have projected them, are no longer fulfilled as they may have been in tribal or medieval societies. The close association of structure and function that existed in simple societies, simply does not hold in advanced societies. The process of structural differentiation, in which separate institutional spheres have developed, has led not only to the eradication of religious involvement in other areas of activity—such as the work order, the status system, the political arena, the operation of law, the organization of education, and the provision of recreation—but also to the loss of the presidency which religion once exercised over practically all of man's doing. Sociologists long ago noticed this development, and, in order to maintain the original idea that religion fulfills necessary functions for society, various explanations of the process have been offered. If religion prescribed the overarching values of society, as some sociologists have suggested, and provided social cohesion and emotional expression, how was the apparent decline of institutional religion accounted for? The answers that have been offered are several.[11] Some have adopted a functionalist *definition* of religion, and have then argued that whatever supplied these functions was, by virtue of

[11] The principal theorist of modern social systems, Talcott Parsons, remained committed to the idea that religion provided the core values of (at least western) modern societies; see Talcott Parsons, *Structure and Process in Modern Societies*, New York: The Free Press, 1960, especially pp. 295–321; idem, 'Christianity and Modern Industrial Society', in E. A. Tiryakian (ed.) *Sociological Theory, Values and Sociocultural Change, New York: The Free Press, 1963;* and idem, 'On the Concept of Value-Commitments', *Sociological Inquiry, 38, 2 (1968), pp. 135–60.*

that fact, religion. Hence, the idea is aired that religion is the celebration of the civic society, or even of the state.[12] We have interpretations that suggest that all man's serious concerns that transcend the strictly biological are to be regarded as religion.[13] And we have the idea that whatever confers a solemn sense of identity on men is religion.[14] My own solution of this problem is somewhat different; and I adopt not a functional, but a substantive, definition of religion, which has the incidental virtue of being in conformity with general usage.

Latent functions and rationalization

The process of social development has, I believe, been a process in which latent functions have been made manifest. In the growth of modern societies a wide variety of activities have become increasingly subject to scientific procedures. Technology, on which we now depend in almost all departments of life, is itself the encapsulation of rational principles. Technology is the attempt to provide the most efficient means for certain given ends, and in the acceptance of new scientific techniques for so many social purposes we have become committed to a highly rationalistic organization of everyday life. One implication of this development is that increasingly we come to look for technical solutions to our problems rather than to rely on the maintenance of particular types of moral attitudes. In the field of social control, we depend less on socializing individuals to given levels of sensitivity, and less on the cultivation of socially useful personality-dispositions; we rely on the operation of mechanical controls. In the west, the virtues which religious commitment entailed, and which were to be rewarded by supernaturally granted benefits, are now less demanded because—it is assumed—the same effects that once ensued from the exercise of private virtues can be much more effectively ensured by the use of public controls. Electronic eyes and data-retrieval systems have largely supplanted inter-personal concern and the deeply implanted virtues of honesty, industry, goodwill, responsibility, and so on. Of course, electronic eyes are expensive, but we have moved to a state of

[12] See Robert N. Bellah, 'Civil Religion in America', in William G. McLoughlin and R. N. Bellah (eds.), *Religion in America*, Boston: Houghton Mifflin, 1968, pp. 3–23.
[13] See Thomas Luckmann, *The Invisible Religion*, New York: Macmillan, 1967.
[14] Hans Mol, op. cit.

dependence on techniques in which we tend to assume that it is always easier to develop new techniques than to return to the long drawn out type of moral education of the past.

Technology demands the development of much more rational modes of thought.[15] The individual today need not be regarded as more intelligent or personally more rational in his thinking than men in the past, but he lives in a world which is increasingly subject to highly rational controls. He must operate with technical equipment. He must obey technical commands. He must be rational in making appropriate responses, and so he is induced by these devices to behave and to think in what is a 'rational' way. If he drives a car, he learns to be rational and to stop when the traffic signals are against him—no matter how urgent his business. The fact that he learns to respond rationally makes it unnecessary to train him in the type of social manners and religious injunctions that told him to 'put others before yourself'; 'behave to others with courtesy and kindness'; and so on. Indeed, were he to behave like that—were he, at the traffic lights, to wave others on ahead of him, even though the lights for him were 'Go' and for them were 'Stop'—he would not only be irrational, but he would disrupt the whole flow of traffic, and probably cause an accident. His courtesy would probably cause him to be arrested; his fault would be that although he had behaved courteously, and even morally, he had not behaved rationally.

In accepting technological controls, the individual learns to use rigorous cause-and-effect thinking in order to cope with the social system of contemporary society—not only in its strictly mechanical aspects, but also in dealing with the bureaucratic machinery that we erect to sort out our social affairs. He is likely to apply this type of thinking increasingly to his own life, and even to areas where there is no direct pressure to think in this way. The consequence is that modes of though that are essentially poetic, symbolic, or aesthetic, which have a significance for the assuaging of the emotions, or for the development

---

[15] The concept of rationality employed here is that of formal, purposive, or instrumental rationality (in contrast to substantive or value-rationality); for discussion of the distinction, see Max Weber, *Wirtschaft und Gesellschaft* Part I, or the English translation, Max Weber, *Theory of Social and Economic Organization* (translated by A. P. Henderson and Talcott Parsons), London: Hodge, 1947, pp. 31ff. For a more technical discussion of some problems involved in the concept, see Bryan R. Wilson (ed.), *Rationality*, Oxford: Blackwell, 1970.

of the inner self, become increasingly alien. At the very least, they have to be compartmentalized, separated from the world of everyday business and public involvements where rational consciousness is essential to cope with prevailing technology. Even in his private affairs, the individual is likely to bring more matter-of-fact attitudes to bear, and to make his judgements in the same terms as those that apply in the socially-organized areas of life.

These consequences, and there are others, all make it much less easy for people to accommodate themselves to two such very different forms of social interpretation as, on the one hand, those presented by modern technology, and on the other hand, that presented by traditional religion. In the self-consciously modernizing context of contemporary society, ancient religious forms appear increasingly incongruous. With the development of international organizations and issues, and universal concepts, any distinctly local tradition comes to represent something limited and apparently un-modern. Not only is the prestige of religious concerns diminished, but they are also relativized by the growing awareness of the diversity of religious movements, and by negative modern appraisals of the effectiveness of religion. In part, the comparison between religion and other social institutions makes apparent the extent to which other institutions have been capable of internal rationalization, while in the case of religion there are distinct limits to the introduction of rational procedures. Thus, whereas all other social institutions can be hierarchized and organized according to the benefits of a division of labour, in which specialist skills can be calculated and conjoined in efficient ways towards the attainment of a particular, empirically specified end, in religion this divorce of means and ends is impossible. The ends are super-empirical; and that the means are efficacious must be accepted as an act of faith. Whereas in law or in education a hierarchy of competence can be established, so that the litigant or the pupil can be dealt with at the appropriate level that his circumstances require—locally for relatively simple requirements, and at a higher level when a strong law or a more developed education is needed—no such sub-division is possible in the provision of the ultimate commodity which religion purveys.

And what is that commodity? It is none of these *latent* functions with which sociologists have been so much concerned.

It is exactly the function which is *manifest* in religion—namely advice about, and training in, the steps necessary for salvation. Salvation is an ultimate concern, and it is the concern of each individual, and the group to which he belongs, or regards himself as belonging. Since salvation is indivisible, and since it must potentially be universally available, religious agencies provide locally what are necessarily recurrent and repetitive patterns of advice and training.[16] The hierarchic division of function obtains only for the organizational and political aspects of the religious system, it does not touch the central concern of salvation. Since religion offers what I shall call 'arbitrary' means of attaining one's end, and since the end cannot be given precise specification (being usually super-empirical) there is a clear limit to the extent to which rational procedures can be adopted for core religious concerns. Religion necessarily speaks another language, offers itself in different terms and by different criteria, from those that prevail in the technological world of modern society.

Contemporary societies function with little recourse to religion as a social institution. If modern states are largely secular in operation, this is because the social arrangements of men are now no longer dependent on the latent functions of religion. As long as social life was basically organized at the level of the local community, religion functioned to sustain the ideational justification, and the emotional and social stability, of the group. But the shift in social organization from the local community to the large-scale society—the process of societalization—has been a process in which the interdependences between individuals and groups, and between the various

---

[16] One of the incidental problems for religion in the modern world is that religious practice—worship or ritual—is necessarily repetitive and needs to be recurrent if men are to have their sense of commitment and allegiance reinforced and renewed, and in order for religion to fulfil its function of providing men with reassurance. Yet, in contemporary life, where much work activity is necessarily routinized, there is a strong tendency, reinforced by the entertainment industry, for men to look to their leisure hours to provide them with excitement and novelty. Obviously, there are great difficulties for the entertainment industry, for example for television, in providing an unending diet of sensation, excitement and novelty (and this, incidentally, may be a factor in the promotion of material that makes ever increasing appeal only to baser animal instincts). At the same time, religion, which must in a sense be always the same, if it is to function both as an agency of solace and socialization, competes on increasingly difficult ground against the various commercial providers of leisure which at least claim to be always offering people new material and new experiences.

institutional and functional arrangements, have been made more explicit and hence more capable of rational articulation. If the large-scale social system operates with little regard to religion as an institution, it also ignores the religious orientations of individuals. The very fact that religion becomes an optional matter, the fact that there is freedom of religion, tolerance, and choice, is an indication that religion is apparently of little direct consequence to the functioning of the social order, at least as that order is understood by those who have helped to build it, modify it, and maintain it. Only a minority of the population attend religious services in many western countries. Even in countries where worshippers are still numerous, as in the United States, it is generally conceded that there has been a process of internal secularization of Christianity, of a kind that has reduced the specifically religious content of religious functions by a very considerable degree. The social system functions without religious legitimation; a large proportion of the population seek only very occasional support from religion, and some never do so at all.

And yet, it is clear that all is far from well with the operation of contemporary society. It is clear that an increasing proportion of people are disturbed by the facelessness of modern bureaucracy, by the impersonality of relationships, and (despite elaborate entertainment and recreation industries) by the sense of boredom that is felt in the manning of the rational technical social system. The social problems of modern society grow at an alarming rate, even though the specific incidence of these problems may vary from one society to another. The growth of crime, of vandalism, and of neurosis and mental breakdown; the growing disruption of marriage; the increase in various types of addiction, whether to drugs, alcohol, or gambling: and the incidence of personal isolation, loneliness, and suicide, all provide a commentary on the points at which the rational social organization apparently fails. Indeed, not only does the system fail to cope with these disruptions, it appears that they arise partly as a consequence of its normal operation.

Religion and contemporary society
The societal system—that is to say the organization of a large-scale advanced society—functions through the articulation of

multiple interconnected role performances, each of which is rationally calculated in its significance and effects. People have to perform these roles, however, and the demands are exacting, while the cultural supports for such performances are not always strong. Discontents with the demands of role-playing become evident because, in the minds of many workers, work and life in modern society have become increasingly divorced from each other. If work becomes drudgery, whilst men are not well-socialized to know how to utilize their leisure time, the cycle of discontent increases. If the meretricious, the merely titillating, the novelties, and the unedifying are increasingly part of the commercial supply of recreational commodities, leisure may cease effectively to refresh and sustain. If the system functions in a way that suggests that everything can be taken care of by the provision of new bureaux, the development of research and social planning, and the further manipulation and state control of incomes and their redistribution, then frustration and ennui are likely to increase. Our very technical competence, and our ability to devise technical solutions, may be in part a source of our problems, since we tend to have faith in new techniques even though there are issues of life which technology cannot resolve.[17]

The social system of advanced societies functions on rational premises. As large-scale, on-going, internally-structured systems, contemporary societies depend on the rational distribution of facilities and resources, and the pressure within such societies is for even greater rationalization. Anomalies, anachronisms, localisms, and individuality become implicit anathema to the system and those who, at every level, control it. Standardization and routinization become values almost in their own right because they facilitate the smooth operation of

[17] We may observe *en passant* how this faith in techniques and 'research' has invaded even the religious sphere. New religious movements in the West sometimes emphasize new therapies which employ what are claimed to be new techniques that have been scientifically discovered. The Church of Scientology is the most prominent movement to make claims of this kind, but there are a variety of quasi-religious therapeutic cults in which magical ideas are backed up with scientific theories; see, for a Japanese example, Winston Davis, *Dojo: Magic and Exorcism in Modern Japan*, Stanford: Stanford University Press, 1980. For these movements, the devices of psychological science, and the rhetoric of natural science (and of science fiction) are easier to deploy than an assemblage of actual scientific equipment. In consequence, mind control is a common emphasis, and so is the representation of the supernatural world in (increasingly familiar) science fiction language. For the latter, see Roy Wallis, 'The Aetherius Society', in Roy Wallis (ed.), *Sectarianism*, London: Peter Owen, 1975, pp. 17–34.

the system. If each man and woman can somehow be reduced to a common level—as a 'labour unit', a 'consumer', or a 'voter'—then they are more easily dealt with by a system that works according to standard calculations, ald in which is sought the greatest precision of planned procedures. The system operates according to values that are themselves predominantly, if not totally, instrumental. *How things shall be done*, not *what shall be done*, becomes the concern of the system, and the idea of ultimate values, or final substantive preferences becomes almost an embarrassment to the assumptions built into the organization of everyday life. True, in politics, at least at election time, voters are given a choice about what should be done, but increasingly the issues become so technical that choice is in fact severely constrained. The choice of what shall be done often resolves itself into simply a choice of which party or which leader shall do *whatever has to be done*—to maintain the system.

Traditional societies often had value systems that were not fully articulated, and which, indeed, often defied articulation. In the religious expressions of a people, these traditional orientations usually acquired elevated and rhetorical formulation, so that men were exhorted to live to do the will of God, or to fulfil the law, or to strive for perfection, or to overcome harmful desire, or to enhance the life of others. These are all substantive values, and it is possible to give them refined expression by reference to a variety of human virtues. But a modern social system is increasingly conceived as operating without virtues; it becomes a neutral, detached, objective, rational co-ordination of role performances. The system induces those who actually man the roles—that is, human beings—to behave as if they had neither virtues nor vices. The pressure is towards the neutralization of human personality, so that roles might be performed with ever greater calculability. Obviously, this pressure from the rational structure is not wholly successful. Nor can it be, since the system depends on human beings to perform roles, and human beings have to be socialized to cultivate dispositions that are moulded for such performances. However, as yet our techniques of socialization are uncertain, and in the particular clusters of attitudes, orientations, and personality dispositions each individual remains unique; none the less, there is no doubt that the pressures within the system are toward the reduction of individuality and towards the organization of men, as uniformly and as mechanically as possible, in segmentary role performances for the sake of efficiency and rational co-ordination.

Modern man, in spite of the benefits of living in an efficient society, and despite his complaints when the system fails in one respect or another, is not wholly content with rational social organization. We all benefit from being treated impersonally and impartially, in experiencing the application of universal abstract principles of justice and fairness, and in knowing that as we move about the world as total strangers, we shall none the less be treated with a basic measure of respect. Yet procedural values do not finally satisfy men, or guarantee them happiness. The rules of how things shall be done leave unsettled the final question of what substantive values are to be subscribed to. Men busy themselves applying the procedural rules, doing this to achieve that, which in turn will become the means to something else, in an infinite linking of rational procedures and efficient techniques. But rationality alone supplies no specific substantive values, other than survival, either for the society or for individuals. And survival, taken just as such, may not be enough.

The social system operates without reference to the supernatural, yet it appears that some individuals periodically find themselves seeking answers or, perhaps more typically, seeking reassurances, which the system as such does not provide. The contingencies of human life occasionally force people to ask fundamental questions about meaning and purpose, and more often to seek support, solace, and reinforcement for their goodwill and commitment. Here, then, might be a place for religion. In itself, this suggests a somewhat private role— religion functioning for individuals. But individuals in unison create groups, and groups may become movements, in which a sense of wider common purpose and subscription to a more substantive philosophy of life might become a focus for large numbers of men. The very aridity of the system's operations and of the assumptions upon which it proceeds may make this type of reassurance, and this acquisition of purposes, all the more attractive. And beyond this, association with the like-minded, and with those who are also impelled to seek fuller satisfactions, and who can form a community of love which quite transcends the impersonal effective neutrality of the social system, may enhance the value of a religious world-view. This substantive concern, this search for positive values must, almost by definition, be religious, since it must invoke something that surpasses the ordinary everyday experience of men. Here, then, we see a function for religion in contemporary society, even though we must allow that it is basically a function for individuals who need to cope with that society, and that the operation of society itself leaves little place for religion, and accords scant appreciation of its potential.

The modern social system operates as if rational principles are in every way sufficient to maintain social organization. And yet men have to be induced to operate that system, to take on roles, and to perform dutifully the tasks assigned to them. The sociologist must ask from what source comes the motivation which induces men to accept these roles? How are human dispositions created, summoned, and mobilized for role performances? Certainly in western societies, the explicit answer to that question is that there is an exchange relationship, an exchange of work for salary. Salary supplies the individual with the means to satisfy his needs and to gratify his appetites. The system works through an appeal to personal gain. Everyone is to make as much as he can. 'Common-sense' for all role performers—employers, workers, or consumers—is 'work for maximum profit' 'get as much as you can'. Because the system is seen as an exchange and because the underlying market assumptions translate time, effort, energy, and skill into monetary terms, there is, at least in western societies, an increasingly inevitable corollary to this maxim—'get as much as you can, for doing as little as you can'. This becomes the conventional wisdom of man in industrial society, the logic of the situation for all factors of production that operate in a rational market situation.

Yet this narrowly conceived idea of exchange, of the interplay of interests, is far from the complete picture. An exposition of the *modus operandi* of the system does not reveal the background assumptions on which the procedure rests. To work at all there must be, behind the exchange relation, a sense of commitment, of obligation, a disinterested goodwill, an attitude of public responsibility and civic virtue. Although the system depends on these things, yet it appears to take little cognizance of them. The western economy of a hundred years ago depended very much on these virtues, and there was widespread awareness of that fact. That was the age of family businesses and owner-managers. It was an age in which relationships were still between persons and not simply between role players. But with the coming of the big corporation and state enterprise, the personal elements have given place to impersonality. For many of those involved in the operation of the system, it is almost possible to assume that personal virtues have become super-fluous because the system works impersonally. The system, increasingly committed to technology, is also increasingly committed to purely procedural values. The agencies which sustain the old-fashioned virtues are unsupported and unrecog-nized. Yet, were these dispositions not widely diffused within the population, were there no residual disinterested goodwill and social obligation, the whole exchange relation would be impossible. Thus there is a paradox: behaviour that appears, when narrowly viewed, to be rational for each individual, and which the system itself promotes, is insufficient, given the nature of humanity, to maintain the basic background conditions for its own operation. There are unexplored elements of 'input' on which a modern society depends but which it does nothing to service.

What, then, is the source of the disinterested goodwill which in spite of itself the system needs if it is to function? In western nations at least, it was supplied in the past by the inculcation of dispositions that were part of a religious world-view. They were stimulated in the natural context of the local community, and steadily broadened to encompass a wider social involvement. They were re-enacted and rekindled, in the context of communal fellowship, shared participation, and caring rela-tionships that have always belonged to some cause higher than the exchange relations of everyday life. They were promoted, in short, in religious activity. In contemporary society, however, the agencies evoking these virtues are weaker, and the agencies that socialized children in these dispositions have fallen into disrepair. Modern society rejects religion on intellectual grounds, and fails to see what the cost might be in terms of the emotional sustenance that men need in order to live. The modern social system operates on implicit assumptions of secularity; in its narrowly conceived rationality, it leaves no room for super-empirical concerns because the relation of these concerns to human well-being is very imperfectly understood, and cannot, in its nature, be subjected to precise rational calculation.

The costs of this tension between religion and rationality in contemporary society already makes itself evident. There is a wide variety of signs of breakdown, which, however, manifest themselves in somewhat different ways in different societies. In Britain, there are strikes and absenteeism on a wide scale, and there is a considerable incidence of vandalism and hooliganism. In America, there is a curious callousness with respect to the impoverished and the disadvantaged, widespread casual violence, and shapelessness in civic and public life. In other countries there is a complete indifference to man's environment and a lack of concern for the conservation of natural resources. In many societies, nothing is now done officially to stimulate civic consciousness. There is a diminution in pride in the wider environment, in public facilities, in the shape and beauty of cities, and in the preservation of the countryside.

Even the facilities, arrangements, procedures, and disposition which constitute the humane and aesthetic culture of a people are increasingly readily sacrificed in the name of efficiency and progress, although this must lead to the ultimate impoverishment of all social life. Unless the basic virtues are serviced, unless men are given a sense of psychic reassurance that transcends the confines of the social system, we may see a time when, for one reason or another, the system itself fails to work, because men lack the basic dispositions to 'give themselves' for the benefit of each other. The conditions for rational work organization may fail, and the background facilities may become so impoverished that men will lose their will to work the social system. Contemporary society operates as if affective-neutrality were a sufficient value-orientation for things to work; it may yet discover that that are other necessities, the virtues nurtured essentially in local communities, in religious contexts, which in the long run will be shown to be as indispensable to the society of the future as they were to the communities of the past.

3

Culture and Religion:
East and West

The role of religion in modern cultures
The general culture of day-to-day life in the advanced nations, whether of the East or West, is not, in modern times, markedly religious. In the past, religion has, of course, been a determining influence on the general contours of those cultures, and contemporary social institutions still exhibit something of the imprint of past religious influences. Traits of individual behaviour and some characteristics of interpersonal relationships evidence persisting, if residual, elements of religious consciousness, and the motivations that are built into the structure of economic, political, and status systems sometimes reveal their old religious roots. Yet, despite the intimacy of the connection of religion and culture in the past, advanced societies—in the very nature of their being advanced—are essentially secular in their operation.[1] That is to say, they are based on secular premises concerning every level of social activity: in their systemic organization; in their economic, political, and social structure; in the values that are explicitly or implicitly espoused; in the texture of relationships; and in the way in which citizens' minds are expected to work; and in the goals that they are likely to pursue.

In western countries, the process of secularization is well documented.[2] Men's diminished concern with the supernatural, and its reduced significance for the organization of contemporary society, illustrates the growing irrelevance to

[1] For an extension of this argument, see Bryan R. Wilson, 'Aspects of Secularization in the West', *Japanese Journal of Religious Studies*, 3, 4, (Dec., 1976) pp. 259–76; and idem, 'The Return of the Sacred', *Journal for the Scientific Study of Religion*, 18, 3, (September, 1979) pp. 268–80.
[2] See David A. Martin, *A General Theory of Secularization*, Oxford: Blackwell, 1978; and Owen Chadwick, *The Secularization of the European Mind in the Nineteenth Century*, Cambridge: Cambridge University Press, 1976.

modern life both of conceptions of a transcendent order and concern with ultimate values. Not least among the causes of religious decline has been the growth in the effectiveness of the modern state in its increased capacity to encompass within its purview, if not directly within its control, ever wider areas of economic and social life. Increasingly, modern society is organized on the assumption that man can manufacture the conditions—at least within certain limits—for social order, for regularity of performances, and for the more exact calculation of production. Whereas at one time monarchs eagerly sought legitimation in religious terms, and particularly so when states were little more than social agglomerations under the leadership of individual potentates, in modern times state power has steadily become either self-justifying or is legitimized, at least rhetorically, by reference to the will of the people. The invocation of any supra-social and supra-political power has become increasingly superfluous. States are, today, in essence secular, even when, in their constitutions or in their traditions, they retain historical allusion to their purportedly religious origins. The state emerges with the development in a large-scale society of effective and centralized co-ordination of power, the controlled distribution of potential force, and an adequately effective system of communication. In that measure in which these things are achieved, so the state may function without the transcendent legitimations that were often necessary in the nascent stages of its growth.

The development of the state has not alone undermined the role of religion in western cultures. The development of science and of philospophical orientations that support it has forced the gradual recession of religious claims to interpret both the natural universe and the social order. The Christian religion itself emphasized logical coherence and non-contradiction, and when to this science added the fruits of empirical enquiry, Christianity became, by virtue of the very logic that it has itself espoused, vulnerable to the findings of scientific discovery. The basis of Christian logic, that one could not simultaneously believe in both 'A' and 'not A', made compartmentalism impossible: one accepted either religious dogma or scientific evidence. Religious authorities increasingly found that they were powerless to restrict scientific investigation, the publication of results, or even effectively to contradict scientific pronouncements. In the conflict, religion became steadily discredited. In astronomy, in physics, in chemistry, and eventually in biology, as these disciplines developed in the West, the certitudes propounded in the name of Christian faith were gradually exposed as untenable. Scientists, philosophers, and even technicians and artisans, first doubted and then disregarded the received religious interpretations of the cosmos, the earth, and of life on the earth. The Christian creation myth was dispelled, and could be retained only as allegory—an allegory the purport of which was often obscure to people who had become accustomed to believing in the literal truth of God's word and the Church's pronouncements.

The growth of state societies and the development of science are but two of the various processes that have led to the alienation of western culture from its religious roots. Yet both the state and science grew from those roots, owing much in their beginnings to Christianity, which, in its own way, can be shown to have recrudescently nurtured a tendency towards secularization. Precisely because it sought to discipline supernaturalism by eliminating all competing religious ideas and symbols, or by absorbing them (and so controlling them), the Church reduced the range, variety, and ubiquity of supernaturalism in everyday life. At its most elevated, it sought to replace local magic with more generalized ethical concerns, and, where it could not attain this, it transmuted particularistic magical orientations by locating them firmly within the Christian scheme, so eventually rendering this immanentist religiosity subject to the ultimately transcendentalist implications of a more abstract, universalistic *Weltanschauung*. The Church's impetus to discipline magic derived from several aspects of Christianity: from the exclusivism that it inherited from Judaism, from its intellectualism and its concern with logic, which it inherited from the Greeks, and from the dogmatic formulations in which the Church claimed to propound definitive statements of truth that were intended to be valid throughout all time and space.

The cultural contours of religion in the West
In contrast with the religions of the Orient, Judaism, Christianity, and Islam has each regarded itself as the only true religion, and this claim to a monopoly of truth has also been made by the major denominations within Christianity.

Whereas in the East there has been extensive tolerance of diverse religious ideas and practices and divergent schools of philosophy, even to the point where one might say that in the Orient it was widely held that the more religion there was, the better, in the West exclusivism has prevailed. Polytheism, as found in Hindu traditions, demands tolerance, of course, and Hindus have been involved in religious conflict principally when faced with less tolerant attitudes of monotheistic religionists, most usually in the encounter with Islam. The Gotama Buddha did not condemn the worship of deities, even though he was pointing to a higher path, and the majority of Theravadin Buddhists worship deities and placate spirits in practice, even though the teachings of their religion counsel quite different activities. The symbiosis of Taoism, Buddhism and Confucianism in China, and of Shinto and Buddhism in Japan, are no less social realities, whatever vicissitudes occurred in governmental sponsorship of one faith or another. In contrast, Jews and Christians were taught to anathematize alien gods, and to regard their worship as false and even demoniac. The Jewish god was, of course, originally a tribal deity, but eventually he came to be conceived as a universal spirit: initially superior to other deities, subsequently he was proclaimed as the only true god. Christians (and in considerable measure, Muslims) inherited this orientation, and there can be no doubt of its powerful influence on western culture.

Exclusivity and the demand that religious dogmas should be logically set out without internal contradictions gave rise in Christianity to a system of theology that was highly intellectual. Logical coherence became a supreme concern of theologians, and they devoted their energies to showing how all knowledge was to be subsumed within the framework of orthodox doctrine. Thus it was that Christians became intensely preoccupied with precise formulations of their sacred teachings. Disagreements about specific items and abstruse metaphysical propositions that lacked every vestige of empirical evidence led to bitter feuds and schisms, with contending parties anathematizing each other. Even so, Christian doctrine combined diverse elements and propositions that were not easily reconciled one with another, including two different eschatological schemes which were so defectively set out in the sacred texts that each became subject to the accretion of extraneous matter and to diverse traditions of exegesis. Given all these hindrances, it was a considerable intellectual attainment to draw together a coherent body of doctrine from a congeries of allegories, myths, parables, moral injunctions, the sometimes dubious historical records of a relatively insignificant group of pastoral tribes, the accounts of their ritual practices, and the sayings of the numerous prophets, all of which were made the background for the doings, sayings and significance of the last of these prophetic figures, who was acclaimed the son of God. To facilitate this intellectual effort, unknown scribes had, at some stage, interpolated false and belated entries in the scriptures to bolster particular theological positions, and these were sometimes retained long after their spurious quality had been abundantly confirmed. The intellectual edifice of Christian teaching was so elaborately constructed and so delicately poised on its scriptural bases that the Roman Church in particular was almost scandalously reluctant to remove even its bogus textual supports. None the less, the long process of systematizing the intellectual foundations of Christian faith was a remarkable enterprise, and so, too, was the application of this body of knowledge to the physical and social world. The attempt to provide a foundation within it from which to interpret all natural phenomena and all social experience—historical, contemporary, and prospective—was for centuries the central preoccupation of Christian philosophy.

This intellectual enterprise may in itself be said to have given a distinct and unifying imprint to the character of western culture, and particularly to the early development of science. Eventually it led to the formulation of a particularly rigorous philosophical approach to the examination and interpretation of nature. These concerns of the intellectual strata affected the general populace very little, of course, but, at that level, the growth of the Church's centralized control over ecclesiastical organization and liturgical practice, its monopoly in licensing priests, and its steady acquisition of economic resources established eventually a degree of commonality in the otherwise somewhat diverse cultures of western nations. Local magic, soothsaying, the recourse to wise men (or women), gave place little by little and unevenly to the acceptance of Christian rites as the necessary means to salvation as being a stronger agency. Formally, the Church taught that rites were not enough, that volition and commitment, belief and faith, were the real requirements for Christian salvation. Slowly (and more impressively after the Reformation) that message had its effect. In the meantime, Christianity itself became the seed-bed of new popular conceptions of the supernatural, and the Church for long did little to disturb the ignorant, vulgar, and quasi-magical conceptions of its power. Instead, the exclusivistic impulse was turned against any lay interpretations of Christian teaching that threatened the Church's power and its claim to a monopoly of truth. Successive waves of heresy occurred, springing sometimes from divergent re-interpretations of doctrine, and sometimes incorporating quite alien systems of thought (as in the influence of Manichean dualism in parts of thirteenth-century Europe). The expectation of the return of the Christian saviour became a popular folk legend in later medieval Europe, giving rise to outbursts of enthusiasm, dissent, and outright rebellion against both Church and king. In this way, the exclusivist claim to a monopoly of truth led not only to the attempt to eradicate competing systems of religious ideology, but also to the categorization as 'heresy' of any form of teaching drawn from Christian doctrine that shifted in emphasis from that which the Church had proclaimed.

Clearly, the exclusivist orientation of Christianity came to operate in the interests of the clerical guild itself. Over the first millennium of Christian history, the clergy had considerably extended their powers, acquiring sacerdotal status as well as total control over doctrine. Had laymen ceased to be convinced of the Church's scheme of salvation, or ceased to believe in the efficacy of the clergy's performances, then the clergy would have lost both the economic support of the laity and their political power. That power rested on their credibility as the proper agents to pronounced on the legitimacy of secular authority, no less than that of religious beliefs and practices. Gradually, persistent and unabsorbed local magic led to the development in the Church of powerful theories of demonology and witchcraft which justified the vigorous attempt to suppress the last vestiges of folk religion in the fifteenth, sixteenth, and seventeenth centuries.[3] More organized lay movements which often drew on the unacclaimed sectarian tradition (support for

[3] See Keith Thomas, *Religion and the Decline of Magic*, London;: Weidenfeld and Nicolson, 1971.

which can easily be found within the Christian scriptures), and the leaders of which usually condemned the corruption among the clergy, were branded as 'heresy', since they constituted an attack on the clerical monopoly of Christian teaching.

That the intellectual exclusivism of Christianity could be so effectively deployed by the clergy was itself a consequence of the close association of the Church and the secular powers. Even before the nascent national states took shape, the Roman Church had acquired the function of legitimizing kings in their office, of superintending public affairs, of pronouncing on the legitimacy of wars, legal actions, and a variety of other public concerns, including the morality of economic activities. Christianity thus came to exercise powerful influence over constitutional, political, judicial, educational, and even economic issues. Since it provided legitimacy to king and state, in return it was able to use the coercive power of the secular arm in the interests of its own monopolistic control of religious activity.

The Church could not have attained its influence over western society, polity, and culture had it not evolved an effective form of internal hierarchic control and a clear structure of authority. This organization was frequently taxed by untoward rebellions, disobedient priests, militant arch-bishops, and negligent popes, and many instances of corruption and abuse, but the structure withstood all these assaults and defections. The Church inherited much of its administrative structure from the Roman Empire, the territory and allegiance of which it in considerable part retained, and this accident of history powerfully affected the Christian religion. Indeed, the history of Christianity has been far too commonly presented from a political perspective, as if the organization of the Church were in itself the history of the religion. The causes for such a bias are easily indicated: the clerics kept the records, and had a virtual monopoly of literacy for some long time, and the common people were paid scant regard. So the political role of the Church, the struggles of popes and kings, and Church and state, and problems of internal Church organization constituted the record, at the expense of concern for the specifically religious aspects of Christianity, the provision of present reassurance of salvation for laymen. Thus it is that our sense of the influence of Christianity on western culture is unlikely to understate the extent of the role of the Church in shaping the formal institutions of culture, and unlikely—for lack of data if for no other reason—to overstate, at least for the pre-Reformation period, the effect of Christian belief and practice on social consciousness. We need to keep in mind this probable imbalance when we acknowledge the advantages that the Church enjoyed in shaping cultural institutions, and particularly such things as the literacy of clerics, the coherence of their interests, and the effectiveness of Church authority and internal discipline. The Church attained a remarkable degree of centralization in a feudal society in which the lack of communication and the limited nature of co-ordination induced the occurrence of spontaneous and recurrent centrifugal tendencies throughout society.

From this position of relative strength, the Church, more than any other agency, provided the inspiration for European high culture. As patron of arts and crafts, most significantly of painting, architecture, and later of music, the Church infused these arts with Christian symbolism, not only promoting the expression of emotion and value, but bringing it under discipline and regulation. Through the arts, religion provided men with a repertoire of emotional expression and an assertion of values, which penetrated all levels of consciousness, so that even everyday speech became affected by religious imagery. Form and structure in the arts were developed to fit religious and liturgical purposes, and although eventually these and other arts broke free from Christian tutelage, the high cultural tradition of western society was initially ordered by it. Folk art continued, of course—some of it (for example, dancing) excluded from Christian contexts, and so from direct Church control, even though the Church sought to ensure moral superintendency of all recreative and festive activity. The Church controlled learning in the universities; it promoted a lingua franca for educational discourse, and had for long a near-monopoly of its use. Its regulation of morals extended even to manners, for it was clerics who produced the manner books to instruct the nobility in the art of public—and private—comportment.[4]. Thus, although regional and local cultures

[4] For a discussion of the influence of books of manners, see Norbert Elias, *Uber den Prozess der Zivilization*, vol. 1, Basel: Haus zum Falken, 1939 (English trans. by Edmund Jephcott, *The Civilizing Process*, Oxford: Blackwell, 1978).

persisted in Europe until the present century, and, in fading measure, do so still, such early unity of culture as Europe acquired came from the agency of the Church. In the industrial era, other unifying forces were to replace the Church in shaping European society, but the seeds of a degree of common consciousness were planted in pre-Reformation times by the Christianity of the Roman Church.

Ideological influences: monotheism and its alternative
All the features of Christianity that I have so far discussed—its exclusivism, its preoccupations with specifically intellectual aspects of religion, its assimilation to political affairs, and its internal organization—appear to lean for support on one other element which emerges as a distinctive characteristic of western religions when they are compared to those of the East— monotheism. The idea of one god, universal and omnipotent, was inherited by Christianity from Judaism, and with it the associated attitudes of exclusivism. The Jewish god,and subsequently the Christian god, would brook no rival, share no platform. But whereas the Jews came, in time, to use religious exclusivism to reinforce ethnic exclusivity, Christians were from the outset a proselytizing people. Their god was exclusive, but they, unlike the Jews, were not an exclusive people. Indeed, the fact that they were competitive, and sought to convert others, made their claims all the more audacious. The distinctiveness of their exclusivism in a world in which men found it easier to accept a plurality of gods, and to subscribe to one or another as their needs occasioned, was responsible for the reputation, and hence, eventually, for the social influence, of Christians. In contrast with other religions, Christianity was regarded by its votaries as a zero-sum proposition: their bid was for total influence, and the risk was total annihilation. When Christianity was adopted by the Roman empire as its official religion, the process of eradicating other gods and their temple became a political concern. The well-being of the empire came to be identified with the success of the Christian Church. Once imperial political power faded, the Church sought to be the guarantor of lesser principalities, and even where this was denied or ignored, its claim to superintend cultural and social life was rarely openly challenged.

Monotheism justified exclusivity. It provided the basis for a clearly formulated system of morality which overrode all local peculiarities and distinctions. Since there was but one god, his will, and thus his law, must be unambiguous, and hence intellectually consistent and coherent, and against it no local departures could be tolerated. The logic of monotheism was that the one god should claim to transcend in power all earthly beings, including emperors, and hence the grace of that god was required to confirm the legitimate title of kings. The one god was set above the plurality of princes, whose duty, so the Church maintained, was to rule as servants of that god. Monotheism justified hierarchy and a chain of authority throughout the Church, which claimed to be the universal church. The logic of monotheism reinforced the aspects of Christianity which made its influence so strong throughout western society. (One ought, in passing, to mention the anti-monotheistic strain within Christianity, and the difficulties of the Church in reconciling the biblical allusions to god, his son, and a holy spirit with the idea of one god. The doctrine of the Trinity and the eventual elevation of the mother of God within the Roman Church, the cult of saints, and even the various depictions of an anti-god or anti-Christ, indicate the difficulty of the struggle of monotheism against the attractions of pluralism, localism, variety, and dualism.)

The features of Christianity to which I have attributed so much of its contribution to western culture all stand in marked contrast to the characteristics of eastern religion. In the first place, whereas Christianity was the primary agency of civilization for most of western Europe outside the confines of the Greek and Roman cities, Buddhism generally was accepted into societies that already had a sophisticated civilization. Thus, the new religion was intruded into older patterns of faith and philosophy to which it necessarily accommodated itself, very evidently, of course, in China.

Secondly, eastern religion has not been marked by an emphasis on exclusivity, and this has had a variety of consequences. Buddhism did not seek to eliminate local deities or local magic, indeed the Gotama Buddha tolerated the worship of local deities, and in Theravada Buddhism deities have a recognizable place, being seen as subject to rebirth and as yet lacking that measure of detachment by which alone they might attain nirvana. All great religions are inclined to become syncretistic at local level, but Buddhism, because of the very tolerance of its stance, was much more vulnerable than Christianity, and neither sought nor attained the same commanding position of political influence. Whereas the Christian Church, once established, escaped the subsequent influence of all other religions, Buddhism made many adaptations, adjusting to local, regional, and national conditions, penetrating Confucian, and later neo-Confucian thought in China, and itself being influenced by it.[5] Even as late as the nineteenth century, when efforts were made—in different parts of Asia and in traditions of Buddhism as divergent as those of China and Ceylon—to produce a Buddhist revival, the revivalists had recourse to strategies and styles of organization that had been imported by their Christian rivals—as in the Young Men's Buddhist Association, and in the publication of popular tracts.[6]

In eastern cultures, diverse conceptions of the super-empirical have been able to co-exist over very long periods of time. Not only was there religious pluralism, in the sense that different cosmologies, different theodicies, and different belief-systems all acquired institutional expression and existed side by side, but the individual himself did not feel the need definitively to decide among them. The very same man who was informed by a sophisticated philosophy and a metaphysical interpretation of life might also be a devotee of some particular local deity, a believer in astrology, or herbalism, or charms, or even witchcraft, or possibly in all of these things. He might add to all this the practice of meditative exercises, and the conviction that spirit possession could occur as a valid manifestation of supernatural power. If men were no less powerfully influenced by religious apprehensions of reality in the East than in the West, they were, however, influenced in more diffuse and less organized directive ways. Christianity sought to take over all other religious influences, and to bring them all into systematic and co-ordinated relationship. Its very lack of tolerance, rather than the power of its intrinsic content, was the source of its penetration of the general social consciousness. The diversified forms of religiosity that have prevailed in the East contrast with

[5] See, for example, the account of Arthur F. Wright, *Buddhism in Chinese History*, Stanford: Stanford University Press, 1959.

[6] For Ceylon, see K. Malalgoda, *Buddhism in Sinhalese Society 1750–1900*, Berkeley and Los Angeles; University of California Press, 1976.

the generally unilinear, directive influence of Christianity on western secular and political consciousness and institutions.

Given the subtlety and complexity of the abstract propositions about both mind and matter that are to be adduced from the Buddha's philosophy, and the much cruder materialistic and concrete account of creation that Christianity inherited, it may seem paradoxical that I should have singled out intellectualism as one of the distinguishing features of Christianity's imprint on western cultures. The contrast relates, however, not to the refinement of a conceptual philosophical scheme as such, but to the extent to which purely intellectual formulations comprise a basic orientation within a religious tradition. Christianity is a religion in which belief—sometimes presented as knowledge, and sometimes required as faith—constitutes the core concern. Jesus demanded faith; the Church came to require intellectual adherence to a number of propositions about God, Jesus, and by extension, humanity and the physical universe. Creed, in its minutely prescribed formulations, became the touchstone of Christianity. When we compare the religions of the East we see—even when, as in Buddhism, a profound philosophical system exists—how much more emphasis is placed on ritual performances and moral injunctions. Of course, these elements are important in Christianity, too, and the Catholic Church increasingly intensified its ritualistic preoccupations in the early centuries, while Protestantism vigorously reiterated man's obligation to obey God's moral law. Yet in both Catholicism and Protestantism the final test was what a man *believed*—his intellectual commitment to a set of doctrinal propositions. Such a demand was made not only of those whom we might call 'intellectuals' or theologians. Articles of belief were frequently issues of popular concern. The scholars, of course, sought to put all phenomena, physical, mental, and social, into the framework of the divine economy as Christian philosophy expounded it, and all this was naturally beyond the common man. None the less, he had to believe in the prescribed articles of faith, and to believe them in the prescribed terms.

In Eastern religions, the formulations of an internally coherent and systematically ordered set of intellectual propositions has not been so predominant a concern either for scholars or for the laity. A variety of sources of wisdom have been acceptable within many eastern cultures, and sometimes within the same religious tradition. Difference of emphasis has been admissible, and even outright contradictions (when assessed on strictly intellectualist criteria) have not necessarily been regarded as detrimental.[7] Diversity in religious styles, and the abundance of varied means to stimulate devotion, have indeed been seen as an evidence of religious vigour. There is, however, another level at which one may indicate the intellectual preoccupations of Christianity when compared to much in the religious traditions of Asia, and this lies in the extent to which emotion—always a powerful substratum in religion—is balanced against the intellect.

Eastern cultures of the Indian sub-continent appear to manifest a much more powerful emotional orientation than those of the West, both in religious and in artistic matters. The western virtue of emotional detachment is less evident in Indian indigenous art forms, including dance and music, and in religion. Whereas western religion sought to discipline and regulate all forms of emotional expression, rejecting dance, eroticism, stimulants, and other ecstasy-inducing substances and procedures as unsuited to religious liturgy, these things have persisted in some branches of Hinduism and in Indian folk religion. The co-ordinated control of the Roman Church in western civilization, and the subsequent puritanism of some of the major denominations of Protestantism, sustained a powerful embargo on ecstatic performance or exercises likely to induce ecstasy. Buddhism, too, sought to regulate emotional expression, but the very tolerance of Buddhist religion permitted the continuance, at the level of folk culture, of emotive expression cast in a broadly religious guise. Thus, whereas in the West activities such as dance became emphatically secular, and often scarcely approved by the Church, in eastern cultures, under Theravada Buddhism, the tendency was for two cultures to emerge within the broad area of religious activity. Thus, a high culture existed that was informed and shaped by élite Buddhism, and below it persisted a folk culture, which, whilst drawing on some Buddhist ideas, amalgamated with them themes and practices drawn from folk art, folk religion, and folk

---

[7] This is immediately apparent of course in the history of Zen Buddhism in which contradiction and paradox, far from being resolved, were elevated into a distinctive feature of religious concern; see Heinrich Dumoulin, *A History of Zen Buddhism*, London: Faber, 1963.

culture. This popular culture was generally despised by the élite, since it hindered, in their eyes, true Buddhist concerns, attaching men to values that were not useful and that did not inspire them to the higher quest. In its pure form, Theravada Buddhist high culture became in part a recluse culture, utilizing painting and sculpture rather than other media of artistic expression, since those other forms were identified with the process of stirring the passions rather than, as in the Theravada ideal, of transcending them. In the West, the arts, or those forms of expression recognized as arts, were drawn very largely into the service of the Church and so were infused with Christian values. The folk art that persisted, in song, dance, story, and in various crafts, steadily lost the associations that it had had with local (pagan) religion, and so was in effect secularized (and sometimes subject to condemnation, or at least to regulation, by Church authorities). In the East, the tolerance of indigenous religion permitted such art to persist in carrying elements of religious import, whether pagan or corrupted Buddhist ideas, even when the spirit of that religion was quite contrary to the ideals of spirituality entertained by the élite.

Cultural transmission: popular and political

The great religions have shaped culture sometimes in quite disparate ways at different social levels. A well-diffused set of religious teachings and practices may influence the social consciousness of particular classes at one particular time, without affecting others, and without influencing the apparatus of the state. A type of religious consciousness might come into being that entirely lacks any institutional expression. Such, for example, was the case with evangelicalism in late eighteenth and nineteenth century England, the theology of which so well fitted the new individualism manifested in economic and social life. But religion may also operate primarily at the formal, political level, perhaps only slowly percolating to the masses; and such cases indeed may be found in the history of all the great religions in one period or another. Or a religion may influence a self-selected élite, who, however, may not see it as their concern either to direct the affairs of state or to engage in proselytizing

---

[8] These points are cogently expressed by E. R. Sarachandra, 'Traditional Values and the Modernization of Buddhist Society: The Case of Ceylon' in Robert N. Bellah (ed.), *Religion and Progress in Modern Asia* New York: The Free Press, 1965, pp. 109–23.

the masses; such in some periods of its history was the case with Buddhism.

The philosophical austerity of a scheme in which salvation was conceived as the transcendence of desire was destined to appeal to a self-chosen order rather than to a mass public, and in this way Theravada Buddhism was socially accommodated. Although all men seek salvation, the Sangha seek it more seriously, each monk for himself. The laity acknowledge the nobility of this goal and accord social esteem to those who pursue it, but the influence of Buddhism, although diffused throughout lay culture, does not so profoundly affect the laity, who do not normally make the same efforts as those made by monks. In countries such as Thailand, where many young men spend at least a short period of their lives as monks, many no doubt carry something of the higher ethos of religion into their subsequent secular lives, but leaving the order implies an abandonment of at least some of the higher demands made of those who would obtain salvation. Merit-making, however readily undertaken by the laity, occurs in the context of a search for other forms of religious or religio-magical reassurance (some of which are also sometimes sought by the monks themselves).[9] The need to make merit becomes an influence on social comportment, and so an agency of social control. No doubt the idea of the bad karmaic effects of misdemeanours may today often be a much debilitated constraint on behaviour (even if not yet as thoroughly weakened as are the comparable Christian concepts of heaven and hell). Yet this constraint still serves to reinforce those general social pressures on a man to seek a good reputation, to maintain social regard, and sustain self-esteem. The need to make merit, in contrast to all other supplicatory and magical devices by which benefits and reassurances might be sought, strengthens religiously-defined social conscience.

The extent to which the popular cultures of Buddhist countries differ as a consequence of the very different soteriological emphases that have come to prevail in the diverging traditions of Theravada and Mayhayana Buddhism is a question to which scholars might give attention. Merit-making

---

[9] For a discussion of Buddhism in Sri Lanka, see Richard Gombrich, *Precept and Practice: Traditional Buddhism in the Rural Highlands of Ceylon*, and also, for Thailand, see Jane Bunnag, *Buddhist Monk, Buddhist Layman*, Cambridge: Cambridge University Press, 1973.

and the emphasis on self-effort in Theravada cultures must imply different consequences for social control and for the internalization of an ethic from those that ensue when religion emphasizes the saving efforts of a bodhisattva, perhaps conveying the implication that the spiritually more advanced have obligations to help others. Standards of social comportment are often to a considerable degree culturally specific, and in the past, if not always today, religious sanctions had a not unimportant part in forming and sustaining the patterns of behaviour in both eastern and western societies. Clearly, other factors are involved—in the Far East, specifically in the development of the secular Confucian ethic which, at least for a class of literati, provided rigorous standards of social behaviour—but a thorough understanding of the determinants of culture would require an investigation of the religious bases of social control and socialization.

The formal level of socialization is institutionalized education, and as a general social institution serving the whole society, education has, in both East and West, been rooted in religion. It was monks and priests who taught in local schools. At higher echelons, the university in the West reflected the emphatically intellectualist orientation of Christianity, opening the way for free enquiry which eventually wrested free from religious sponsorship and influence the various academic disciplines. The concern for logical coherence of argument and (under Puritanism) with mastery of the physical world, led to intellectual systems which broke free from formalism and dogma. The process was eventually reflected at the school level, as rote learning and moral content were steadily replaced by open enquiry and technical competences. General education initially included a largely religious content in the West, but became increasingly secular—without, however, becoming anti-religious or secularist in ideology. The contrast of schooling in the monastery schools of Theravada Buddhist countries and that of western countries in the century immediately before the Second World War indicates a significant difference in the influence of religion on general culture. Since then, of course, the westernization of education throughout the world has led to the steady erosion of religious influence, of whatever kind, at the level of general education.

Religion may put its imprint on culture not only by, or not so much by, forging or controlling the consciousness of the people, but by shaping the instruments of the state. In eastern religions, this influence on the state and its institutions did not attain—even in the case of Asoka, who wished to further the cause of Buddhism by political means—the level of sustained and institutionalized influence achieved by Christianity. The separation of Buddhist concerns from those of the everyday world must always compromise a Theravada Buddhist theory of political science. If nirvana is man's goal, then the religion that canvasses such a goal can scarcely concern itself with the issues of ordering the mundane society. The ideal monk, as a recluse, was not mindful of the relative merits or demerits of particular polities, strategies, or worldly goals; he was unavailable to statesmen, even had they wanted his advice.[10] Until the impact, in relatively recent times, of nationalism, anti-colonialism, social welfare concerns, and the international clash of ideologies, monks did not offer Buddhist teaching as a basis for social and political action. But if pure doctrine disallowed involvement, none the less, in Ceylon and Thailand, the sangha has had a special relationship with the monarchy, and at times, Buddhist teaching notwithstanding, the sangha has been a political force. Yet all of this has occurred without the complex formal ties of church and state that occurred in the western case. Similarly, in Mahayana Buddhism in Japan, we can distinguish between the willingness of monks to serve the political authorities, and their search for political influence, from the more formalized connexions of church and state which characterized Christianity for so much of its history.

The virtual inextricability of religious and political institutions in Islamic culture; the close parallelism of church and state in Christianity with the development of a politically-organized church structure; and the separation of religion and the state in Buddhism (informal links and influence notwithstanding) represent three divergent patterns of association. Clearly, wherever there is a concentration of power and influence in the religious sphere, there is a likelihood of some measure of association (and some might say collusion) between

[10] This was, of course, an ideal; in practice, monks in Theravada Buddhist countries were not always remote from political activity, especially in matters concerning the sangha, any more than were Japanese Buddhist monks in periods when the court was susceptible to their influence.

those who claim spiritual power, and those who wield temporal power. Religion has always the potential to further political causes, if in nothing else, then in the maintenance of order and in the possibility of inducing men to exert—in what are offered as their own long-term interests—restraint and self-control. Supreme temporal power has commonly looked to religious legitimation as a reinforcement of its claims, even when it has done so without direct institutionalization of that legitimation (such as occurred in the Christian case). Some scholars have, indeed, claimed Buddhist legitimation for kingship in the concept in Theravada Buddhism of the *cakkavatti*, or world ruler, who is assimilated to the ideal of a bodhisattva.[11] But, whatever judgement may be made by specialists on this thesis of Theravada political science, even its exponent concedes that the dharma of the righteous ruler is encompassed within the dharma as cosmic law and truth, the way to which is the renunciation of the world.

Organizational influences

Ultimately, of course, the ascetic interpretation of the demands of the founders of both Buddhism and Christianity would contravert worldly involvements, and most particularly so at the level of worldly authority; but, in practice, religion accommodates political power. The cultural consequences of such accommodation are, at least partially, mediated by the coherence of the theories and the logic of the arguments by which such a compromise with the total authority of the original religious pronouncements is achieved. Christianity, as we have seen, was accomplished in this respect, and the theory of the operation of the relative natural law justified the Church in legitimizing both political authority and the existing economic organization of the social order.[12] Such theories and arguments, of course, in turn need a well articulated organizational structure to sustain them. Discipline within the religious

[11] This argument is developed by S. J. Tambiah, *World Conqueror and World Renouncer: A Study of Buddhism and Polity in Thailand against a Historical Background*, Cambridge: Cambridge University Press, 1976.

[12] Catholic theologians argued that under natural law perfect justice and equality would prevail, but since man was in a fallen state, in the present condition of the world injustices persist. The role of the Church in this period (regarded as an interim before God's law is restored) is to exhort the rich and powerful to behave with mercy and charity, and to persuade the poor to be content with their lot in the knowledge that when God again judges man the righteous will be rewarded.

guild, lines of clear authority, and the emergence of figures of authority who validate the application of doctrine to contemporary social and political issues. Hinduism obviously never acquired such formality of organization, lacking even the mechanisms by which a cohesive self-disciplined guild of religious functionaries might be maintained as a guild, but relied on more diffuse patterns of control. Brahmins functioned locally, and whilst their services to laymen were everywhere available, they were not in any sense centrally organized. In Buddhism, the framework of order existed within the sangha, of course, but the sangha was never a parochial clergy. Neither any individual monk nor the local community of monks regarded the laity as their responsibility, as their 'charge' to use the term common in Christianity. The sangha had mechanisms of discipline, but its organizational concerns were internal, and its operation more that of a community than of an articulated role-structure. Even the reorganization of the sangha in nineteenth century Thailand, when a national hierarchy was instituted with a co-ordinated and graduated system of control from regions, provinces, and districts down to local communities, left the sangha concerned essentially with its own self-administration; nothing like a parochial pattern was created.[13] The Thai system, too, depends on agencies of state, and from the state borrows both form and warrant; the sangha has no independent authority outside its own affairs, and it is not capable of influencing the state polity; rather, indeed, it has itself been moulded by the organization of the reformed state.

The Buddhist revival of the late nineteenth century throughout the Orient led to the development of a variety of new structures in both Theravada and Mahayana countries, and there were attempts to create closer ties—ecumenism of a kind—among the various branches of Buddhism.[14] Given the measure of toleration for which Buddhists are celebrated, such a development might have appeared to be distinctly possible, and yet, for lack of an international authority, and of rational organization within each Buddhist country, little came of these endeavours. The organizations that were set up, such as the

---

[13] On the organization of Buddhism in Thailand, see Kenneth E. Wells, *Thai Buddhism: Its Rites and Activities*, Bangkok: published by the author, 1960.

[14] See A. F. Wright, op. cit., pp. 110ff; for a general discussion, see K. Malagoda, op. cit.

YMBA and groups in various countries that made it their particular mission to promote Buddhism by more systematic means, took on styles borrowed from the western world, and often styles specifically evolved within the Christian Church. In Theravada Buddhism in particular, the division of the sangha and the laity remains prominent, and given the philosophical position of Theravadins it is difficult to see how it could be otherwise, even though the Buddhist Commission in Ceylon in 1954 recognized, in the words of Donald E. Smith, 'the pressing need for the creation of a coherent Buddhist organization which would link together the Sangha and the laity in an organized relationship. What was needed, in short, was a Buddhist church.'[15]

The contrasting features of eastern and western religion are, in considerable measure, correlated with or subsumed in the difference between monotheistic and what may loosely be called pantheistic orientations. Monotheism makes for exclusivity and control. It justifies hierarchy, and provides a rationale for the co-ordination of activities to serve one supreme end, for which temporal monarchy has often been a model. In contrast, pantheism accommodates to diversity of phenomena, and from it specific categories of natural order are perhaps less readiy generated. Conceptions of a supreme purpose or an ultimate goal, as in unity with Brahma in Hinduism, or attainment of nirvana in Buddhism, have not functioned in the same way as the supreme deity of monotheistic systems. Sociologically, they are of less importance than the fact that these goals accommodate in everyday life the polytheistic tendencies of localism. Such hospitality to a plurality of gods merges easily into syncretism, and this process characterizes the history of Buddhism in diverse ways in both its northern and southern migrations. A pantheistic orientation facilitates the acceptance of quite divergent representations of religious truth, not even the contradictions among which are regarded as particularly detrimental; each representation reflects the many partial apprehensions of ultimate reality manifested everywhere in the natural, and potentially also in the social, world.

These tendencies clearly circumscribe the extent to which

---

[15] Donald E. Smith, 'The Sinhalese Buddhist Revolution', pp. 453 88 in Donald E. Smith (ed.), *South Asian Politics and Religion* (p. 474), Princeton: Princeton University Press, 1966.

any one predominant tradition can shape society and culture; when a particular religious tradition accommodates others, or tolerates divergence or contradiction, its influence on cultural phenomena becomes muted. The jealous god of Judaism, and subsequently of Christianity and Islam, provided directives for everyday life that brooked no compromise. God's will became the prescription for social order, deviation from which became at least heretical and possibly devilish. In comparison, eastern religions provided no such social dynamic. The passivity of Buddhism and the indeterminacy and tolerance of Hinduism, and the lack of sustained zeal in proselytizing, appear to bear a relationship to the absence of that rigour which monotheism has encouraged in western religion.

In assessing the relation of religion to culture we are necessarily concerned with what has been called practical religion, that is religion as it is made socially manifest, the religion of villagers and householders, and, in latter days, of city clerks and industrial workers.[16] When we take this practical religion, and not the elevated notions of the sacred texts, as the basis for analysis, we see that both Hinduism and Buddhism, despite the elevated transcendental conceptions of their formal doctrines, give rise in practice to essentially immanentist religiosity. The contrast with Christianity is evident: in continuity with its Judaic predecessor, Christianity has succeeded, much more than oriental religions, in sustaining a transcendentalist perspective. This is not to suggest that there have not been examples in Christendom of the periodic resurgence of immanentism, from the lingering cults of ancient local deities (sometimes born anew as saints of the Catholic Church) in the Middle Ages, to the contemporary enthusiasm for charismatic renewal, manifested in the phenomenon of glossolalia.[17] But in general, the effectiveness of Church organization and control has been such that untoward evidences of the operation of divine and supernatural forces at work in the world have been subject to rigorous scrutiny. The Roman

---

[16] The term 'practical religion' is used by Edmund R. Leach (ed.), *Dialectic in Practical Religion*, Cambridge: Cambridge University Press, 1968.

[17] There is now an extensive literature on the Charismatic Renewal movement; for the movement within Catholicism, see, for example Killian McDonnell, 'The Catholic Charismatic Renewal: Reappraisal and Critique', *Religion in Life* (Summer 1975), pp. 138–54; and for a more general account, Richard Quebedeaux, *The New Charismatics*, New York: Doubleday, 1976.

Church has become very slow to admit new candidates for canonization, and scrupulous in subjecting claims of the miraculous to scientific test; the possibility of the immanent operation of the divine is not denied, but the Church is increasingly sceptical. In general, even though God is still thought to be susceptible to human dispositions and supplications, divine power is not expected to be manifest in the world: nature and supernature are markedly distinct. The world is profane—and, in the Christian conception, sullied by sin—and the deity, remote from this profanity, may be reached only because of his mercy.

The distinction of immanent and transcendental conceptions—borrowed from Christian theology—allows us to indicate some facets of the divergent emphases between eastern and western cultures, but the terms do not, of course, dichotomize the religion of East and West, within which there has been and remains considerable diversity. Whilst transcendentalism has been a more potent force, and has been more successfully sustained in Christianity than in Buddhism, none the less, in the concept of nirvana, Theravada Buddhism maintains a far more elevated transcendentalist perspective than that of any other religion. Perhaps, indeed, because of this extreme transcendence, Theravada Buddhism is rarely found practised in its pure form—a form consistent with its basic canon. When a religious system embraces ideals which too far transcend the day-to-day experience of ordinary believers, and when its conceptualization passes beyond normal comprehension, we may expect that men will find other resources to cope with their immediate problems and their search for security. The transcendental character of pure Theravada Buddhism led to the consequence of inducing men to turn to other sources of religious reassurance: that of Christianity (where alternative and lesser sources of spiritual help were inadmissible, especially in Protestantism) led to secularization. In Puritanism, the deity became so remote from everyday life that for the man-in-the-street he was virtually expelled altogether from the working of the world, and so, for most people, from the individual's consciousness.

The reformations of tradition

Periodically within particular cultures, great reformations, revivals, or diffusions of religion have profound effects, which become more specifically determining of subsequent social development than was the earlier religious tradition. Such an occasion in Japan was the arrival and spread of Buddhism; and such an instance in western Europe was the Protestant Reformation and its aftermath. It would be foolhardy for me to attempt to discuss, were I indeed able, the many aspects of Buddhism in Japan, but it is perhaps true to say that Buddhism provided for Japan a much more universalistic orientation than had previously been available in the indigenous Shinto tradition. That orientation was, at times, and particularly under the Tokagawa Shogunate, limited to a national perspective. But a national perspective—itself perhaps more easily attained but also less easily transcended in the Japanese case— might be seen as a step towards universalism, and certainly this was so in Christian countries of the West. Japanese Buddhism emphasized the practical orientations of an active immanentist faith, and implicit in the idea that all men might attain salvation there lies, of course, a powerful stimulus to universalism. Different schools presented this universal prospect in different ways, but there is to be observed something of a progression towards more complete ideas of compassion and mutual help—an ethical striving in this world, which differed from the emphasis characteristic of Theravada Buddhism, in its pure doctrinal form, on contemplation and the overcoming of desire towards the attainment of nirvana. The this-worldly orientation manifest in Japanese Buddhism may be one of the roots of a positive inducement towards work in this world for the upbuilding of human society.

Protestantism in Europe was equally a re-direction of man's energies towards this-worldly concerns. In place of the other-worldy orientations of the monk in mediaeval Catholicism, Protestantism, and most explicitly Puritanism, directed men to work in this world with the psychological inducement that their task was the mastery of worldly things, and their obligation was to work in their callings.[18] Calvinists maintained that although

[18] The *locus classicus* for this thesis is Max Weber, *The Protestant Ethic and the spirit of Capitalism* (English translation by Talcott Parsons), London: Allen and Unwin, 1930; see also idem, *The Sociology of Religion* (English translation by Ephraim Fischoff), London: Methuen, 1963. For a particularly interesting re-working of the Weber theses in a context in which they have not previously been fully examined, see Gordon Marshall, *Presbyteries and Profits*, Oxford: Clarendon Press, 1980.

a man could not positively claim that he was destined to post-mortem glory as one of God's elect, none the less, he was equally not to doubt it. This fine line between not asserting and not doubting one's salvation was seen by Weber as a crucial cultural determinant of western psychology. It led to the informal assumption among Puritans that success in his calling in this world was an intimation of the individual's prospects in the next. Thus was established a psychological mechanism that promoted the work ethic and directed men to the goal of achievement.

The formulation of an ascetic ethic, in which the ordinary layman accepted his social obligations in the same spirit as had the monks of medieval Catholicism, called for the elimination of the spiritual division of labour which Catholicism had supported. For Calvinists, there were now to be no specialist religious virtuosi—all men were to lead the solemn and dedicated religious life, and were to do so in the secular world, achieving things for the glory of God, and for the psychological reassurance that such success intimated (in their vision of things) with respect to their prospects in the after-life. The moral law ceased to be a debit-and-credit account of bad deeds and good works; the devout Christian was now to do good not in the *expectation* of reward, but because this was the law of his god, who could not be bribed by man's behaviour. He was, above all, to be his own judge, and to answer to his own conscience. No priests could intercede for him, and no rituals could affect his condition. The transcendent god had already predisposed man's destiny, and to alter this a man could do nothing. The demand for an internal standard of moral behaviour was, of course, culturally transformative of western society. Individuals had now an obligation to observe their own conduct carefully, to walk seriously, in the full consciousness that they were God's instruments, with moral obligations to all mankind. This powerful demand for new levels of self-control was the basis for the new work order which burgeoned under capitalism. It was also the beginning of man's acquaintance with the idea that he should depend upon himself, and indeed had so to depend, since God was no longer active in the world, and the church had no role save that of teaching God's law and of offering men spiritual guidance. One might say that the drama had been written, and men were simply to act it out according to the best counsel they could obtain, and in the light of their own consciences.

Among the consequences of Protestantism, and more especially of Puritanism, was the impetus that the new faiths gave to active work in the world, and so to science. Mastery of the universe was what God has bequeathed to man, and, in his calling, man was to demonstrate the glory of God by discovering the wonders of the physical world, just as he was to maintain the standards of the saints in his moral life. Mastery was a key concept, and so Puritanism was entirely conducive to the promotion of science.[19] Science had its own consequences for man's religious orientations: it became, in time, one of the principal factors in setting Christian religion at a discount. Similarly, in the development of capitalism, Puritanism acted as something of a pump-priming mechanism, releasing energies in new forms of enterprise, and stimulating men to seek achievement. Initially, men sought personal reassurance of their worth in the eyes of God by their worldly success. In the course of a very few decades, capitalism had acquired its own rationale, and achievement had become its own end, without further thought of what it intimated about the divine will. What, under Puritanism, had been a stimulus to action that Weber described as substantively rational, in that it was action which had a given, arbitrary end (the glory of God), became, under capitalism, essentially action of a formally rational kind, in which every end was merely the means to some less proximate end. The process was, of course, a religiously inspired transformation of culture.

Puritanism was, then, a catalyst, facilitating the development of an entirely new economic and scientific culture in western nations. As Weber sought to show, the spirit of capitalism was already evident in Benjamin Franklin in America whilst that country was still no more than an agrarian society, and even though Franklin was himself far from being a Puritan. One might argue that despite the limits of its economic development, the scientific spirit was equally an autonomous force in America, and Franklin might just as easily be taken as an

---

[19] For a cogent early statement of the relationship between Puritanism and science, and the stimulus for an extensive subsequent literature, see Robert Merton, *Social Theory and Social Structure*, Glencoe, Ill.: The Free Press, 2nd edn., 1957, chapter XVIII pp. 574–606.

example. The spirit of capitalism and the spirit of science, freed from their religious mentor, have become independent parts of the ethos of western society. The religious reformation, to which they owed their existence, became a diminished force, but the culture of western society was now transformed.

The Puritan reformation affected principally the mercantile and bourgeois classes of western society. Later, many elements of the spirit of that reformation were to re-emerge, in somewhat transmogrified form, and directed to different classes of society in England, which was of course the first nation to become industrialized, in the shape of the Methodist revival. Methodism powerfully re-expressed the work ethic to the lower stratum of the population. Its gospel emphasized the virtues that go into the making of a man dedicated to work in the increasingly impersonal context of capitalist society—industriousness, conscientiousness, willingness, frugality, seriousness of mind, sobriety, and punctuality. Appropriately, given the wider population of the less educated classes to which this new evangelical form of Christianity was to appeal, Methodism's doctrine was very different from the Calvinist thesis of predestination, according to which a man's afterlife fate, whether of salvation or damnation, had been sealed by God from time immemorial. Whereas Calvinism embraced the psychology of an élite, which combined a democratic polity in their own church with the aristocratic ideal of being God's putative elect, Methodism operated according to a psychology much better fitted to the labouring masses. In church polity, Methodism (under Wesley and his successors) was essentially autocratic; but with respect to the promise of salvation in the life hereafter, it was democratic to the point of being demotic. Man's free will to choose salvation was its essential emphasis. Not only could a man choose the path of salvation, but in an appeal of even cruder directness to potential converts, Methodism also taught that a man could also be *assured* that he was already saved. Yet, if the psychology of the two movements was different, the effect in disseminating a work ethic was similar: Methodism was responsible for diffusing serious habits of work through the working population of the Anglo-Saxon world.

The gradual expansion of the prospects of salvation is not an uncommon phenomenon in the history of religion. Indeed, although there are long periods in the course of religious development when ritual procedures, formal doctrines, and social organization become more and more elaborated, institutionalized, and increasingly the closed monopoly of clerical castes, there can also be noted instances in which new movements arise that seek to cut through the accretions of ritual, doctrine, and organization, to provide swifter ways to salvation—that is, sociologically speaking, swifter ways to the reassurance that men seek from spiritual sources. In this process, more rational procedures and structures, and less complicated doctrines, represent laicizing tendencies; the prospects of salvation are opened up to a wider public.[20] It might be instructive, with propositions of this type in mind, to examine the admittedly multi-faceted and far from unilinear history of Buddhism in Japan. Certainly, there are instances in Japan of different and successive sects expanding the prospects of salvation for men, until such an outcome has become virtually a universal possibility.[21] In emphasizing man's dependence for salvation by rebirth into the Pure Land on faith in the Amida Buddha, the Jodo Shu sect has certain resemblances to the evangelical Arminianism that became popular once the rigours of the Reformation had waned among Protestants; everyone might claim salvation through the efforts of a saviour. Jodu Shinshu took the process a step further, again in a development that reminds one of certain Christian movements, in declaring that everyone was already saved, even if unaware of it. The Universalists, among Christian denominations, adopted a not dissimilar position, and in Mormonism and Christian Science there is also an undercurrent of a similar universalism: everyone is likely to be saved.

[20] The two processes briefly indicated here are, of course, the subject of an extensive literature, but the rhythms between the forces of institutionalization and cultural accretion on the one hand, and those iconoclasm and systematic disavowal on the other, have yet to be given adequate attention. Some preliminary suggestions may be found in T. F. O'Dea, 'Five Dilemmas in the Institutionalization of Religion', *Social Compass*, 7, 1, (1960), pp. 61–7; B. R. Wilson, 'American Religion: Its Impact on Britain', in A. N. J. den Hollander (ed.), *Contagious Conflict: The Impact of American Dissent on European Life*, Leiden, E. J. Brill, 1973, pp. 233–63; B. R. Wilson, 'American Religious Sects in Europe', in C. W. E. Bigsby (ed.), *Superculture: American Popular Culture and Europe*, London: Paul Elek, 1975, pp. 107–22.

[21] Of course, among intellectual strata, ideas such as that of universal salvation are of ancient provenance, but it appears that this did not give rise to distinct popular religious movements. As ideas they may be found among the early proponents of Zen Buddhism in China centuries before they became articulated in new popular movements.

The secularizing impulse

Whatever the influences that religious traditions may have exerted on eastern and western cultures in the past, in the modern world there appears to be a virtually universal process in which the social influence of religion diminishes—a process known to sociologists as secularization. In the different historical contexts of eastern and western cultures, divergent specific causes have no doubt been active in the precise course by which religion has lost its social significance. The decline of western religion has been associated with the emergence of new and more powerful influences on the shape of western culture, in particular the two agencies that we have already mentioned: the growth of science and the development of the state. It might also be argued that the specific course of religious change itself not only accommodated the nascent tendencies towards a more secular society, but in certain respects also stimulated that process. Protestantism was a reform of Christianity which promoted very considerable rationalization both of religious ideas and of everyday life. It did so by reducing the plethora of powers to which popular Catholicism subscribed. In its vigorous transcendentalism, it eliminated the remaining im-manentist elements that had survived in the Roman Church. Magical intercessions, special places of holiness, relics, and shrines were all condemned. The magical interpretation of the sacraments was abrogated. Rituals were henceforth to be regarded more as memorials than as acts that manifested intrinsic power. In the early centuries of Christianity, Roman priests had steadily acquired attributions of mystic power, and their role had become intensely sacerdotal. The reformers rejected sacerdotalism and the mystical claims that had come to characterize the style and performances of the Roman clergy. The priesthood and its functions became demystified—reduced to the role of ministry. The Protestants abolished clerical celibacy, which in the Catholic Church had reinforced the clergy's claim to special status, and which hd contributed to the sense of sanctity that the priesthood had cultivated. The elimination of clerical celibacy had parallels, of course, in the development of Japanese Buddhism, and represents a signifi-cant step in the process of demystification. The acceptance, in the Methodist movement, more than two hundred and thirty years later, of a lay ministry, organized to work alongside those fully ordained as clergy, was a continuation of the same general trend. Ritual and priesthood although strongly defended in the later nineteenth century as the authentic institutions of Christian organization, and as indispensable elements for worship, gradually became of diminished significance. New emphasis on other aspects of the clergy's functions led to a more professional style, in which pastoral care, group leadership, church management, and informal association have somewhat displaced older preoccupations with worship and liturgical detail. In the light of contemporary theological reinterpretations of the priest's role and the abandonment, since 1962, of many of the erstwhile claims for priesthood and liturgy in the Roman Church, the earlier (Nineteenth and early twentieth century) ritualistic and liturgal revivals in both Catholicism and Anglicanism can be seen to have been no more than passing and perhaps misplaced reactions against the dominant longer-term currents in western religious history, especially as initially manifested in Protestantism.[22]

The laicization and incipient rationalization that have occurred in Christianity is wholly consonant with the steadily growing influence of science and technology in western cultures generally, and with the way in which society itself has been systematically re-organized. The course of development has, of course, been uneven, but in the third quarter of the twentieth century there has been a dramatic turn-about in the policies of even the Roman Church from ritualistic to increasingly rational principles of operation. Instrumental values and the accompanying attitudes of mind, having become the dominant mode of western culture, have exerted their influence on religion, which, instead of shaping secular values, as once in large part it did, is now increasingly shaped by them.

The tradition of Mahayana Buddhism has always carried the potential of encouraging lay involvement to a much greater degree than has been the case with Theravada Buddhism. It has been more hospitable to the practical orientations necessary for life in the secular society, and, even if, at local level, it has often been vitiated by an accommodation of folk religion and magical concerns, it has not been alien to the cultivation of a secular work ethic. The ideal of putting the well-being of others

---

[22] Catholic commentators have not hesitated to describe recent changes in their own church as 'protestantization'.

before the gratification of one's own desires is an injunction that contains the seed of strong attitudes of social and civic responsibility, and these must influence secular life. What Mahayana Buddhism lacked, of course, was the orientation to exclusivity with which to contend against contrary religious and secular values. It lacked the organizational structure that would have enabled it to censure contrary dispositions and to reinforce its own ethical prescriptions. And it has no adequate political expression or even appropriate formulae that could be adopted easily by the national state society. Yet there is an interesting paradox in the Mahayana case. The doctrine of karma, at least as popularly conceived, provides the possibility that, by reference to it, men will find for themselves excuses for their immediate moral and material failings. The parallel with the sociologically equivalent technique of escape from an ethic of responsibility that is provided (in practice, albeit not in its theological intention) by confession of sins to a priest in Roman Catholicism, is immediately apparent. Each case provides excuse. Yet when, even on only a cursory acquaintance, we compare the evidence of an ethic of social and moral responsibility, for instance in Japan, and the extent to which such an ethic is lacking in Roman Catholic countries, the cultural contrast is striking. Does the maintenance of so high a standard of civic responsibility among the Japanese (a fact that led one distinguished British economist to call them, 'the greatest nation in the world'[23]) stem from Buddhism, or indeed from any other religious influences on national character and culture?

We have well-developed theories of the influence of Protestantism on the creation of a work ethic and an attendant quality of civic morality in the countries of western and northern Europe, but the Japanese case, which has some intrinsically similar (if also many different) features, cries out for full sociological analysis.[24] Certainly one sees, in the resurgence of modern mass Buddhism in the new religious

[23] The phrase was used by Sir Roy Harrod, as quoted by E. H. Phelps Brown, 'Sir Roy Harrod—A Memoir', *Economic Journal*, 90, 375 (March 1980), p. 32.

[24] The search for a cultural agency in Asia that corresponded in its influence and effect to the Protestant ethic in Europe has stimulated various studies: see Robert N. Bellah, 'Reflections on the Protestant Ethic Analogy in Asia', *The Journal of Social Issues*, 19, 1963, pp. 52–60; R. N. Bellah, *Religion and Progress in Modern Asia*, New York: The Free Press, 1965; S. N. Eisenstadt (ed.), *The Protestant Ethic and Modernization: A Comparative View*, New York: Basic Books, 1968, Part iii, pp. 243–383.

movements in Japan, the conscious, articulate, and vigorous reassertion of such values, and these movements no doubt sustain in the modern period the impulses of a strong ethic of responsibility. Yet the origins of that ethic are, to me, very far from clear.

The culture of the secular societies of our own times—societies organized increasingly on rational principles, devoted to planned empirical goals, and legitimized by reference to the will of the people and not to any transcendent entity or state—may still bear the strong imprint of the religious teachings of past centuries on the mental dispositions of the people and in persisting institutions. The mentality of the people of an alien culture remains to all of us in some degree a mystery, even when we command their language. And this is so even of societies with which our own shares some considerable part of the same cultural inheritance, and some of these differences are attributable to differences in religious history. In Europe, the difference between Catholic and Protestant countries or regions is immediately evident, even in societies in which religion now has only a shadow of the influence that it once enjoyed. Even between Protestant countries that have been committed to different branches of Protestantism—and such is the case, for example, with England and Scotland—the cultural deposit of these divergent religious perspectives is still readily apparent in a wide variety of everyday cultural phenomena. There are, obviously, many specific sources of such contemporary differences, but one significant variable is the disposition, among the many that can be identified within any one significant religious tradition, which prevailed in formative periods of secular history. Different Christian theologians sustained distinctive attitudes to secular culture which might be traced through particular Church élites. In some periods, the Church authorities saw religion as utterly transcending the secular culture; at other times, as standing opposed to it; and in yet other instances as being the fullest expression of the secular world.[25] Yet, despite all the differences internal to a religion which affect the secular culture, it is still possible to indicate, at least in very broad terms, some of the general features that are significant *tout court* in the history of a religion's influence on

---

[25] For a discussion of these different orientations in the work of various Christian theologians, see H. Richard Niebuhr, *Christ and Culture*, New York; Harper, 1951.

secular society. I think that there are general features in Christianity, that have had persisting influence in the culture of the West, and I should like briefly to contrast the most significant of these with the situation, as I understand it, in eastern countries.

The nature of social control

Perhaps the most explicit preoccupation that is generally common to Christianity in all its traditional variants is the concept of sin. Christian theology defines man as innately sinful; his sinfulness is, in some way, supposed to be genetically carried from the original sin of Adam, the first man, who disobeyed God. That original sin lay in sexuality, and man's carnal nature, from which all specific human defects stem, is attributed to man's acceptance of the temptation of the devil at the very beginning of his existence. It follows that the Christian is always guilty. He is guilty because he is a man. Christianity teaches the frailty of human kind, and in Catholicism, in particular, it was stressed that man could not escape sin, and, in consequence, would necessarily be punished in the life after death until he had discharged his sinful debts. The moral economy of Christian theology is that Jesus Christ came as a saviour to save men from the final consequence of sin—which has been variously re-presented either as eternal torment in hell or as death. Christ's act of sacrifice was to save men from the full consequence of sin, to redeem him, although in traditional Catholic thought man would not altogether escape without some measure of punishment. That he had even an eventual hope of attaining paradise was due, after confession of his sins, only to Christ's intercession on his behalf. Clearly, in the background of this scheme of things is the Judaic Old Testament conception of God as a stern father, always ready to punish his disobedient people, always seeking retribution.

   In the Christianization of European culture, this concept of sin was quickly built into a system of social control in which the Church's concern with the moral behaviour of man was easily associated with the demand of secular authorities for obedience and social order. The Church became the guardian of public propriety, providing kings and states with a supernatural legitimation for the demands that they made for the good behviour of the people. What the Church defined as sinful acts, the secular authorities often regarded as illegal acts, and individuals were faced with the prospect of public punishment for such acts as well as needing to maintain self-control by the burden of an inculcated sense of guilt. This process of internalization of conscience was very much accelerated by the Reformation, and more particularly by Calvinism. Since private confession to priests was abrogated, a man became the keeper of his own conscience, and thus the balance of regulation shifted from the agencies of social control increasingly to dependence on the individual's own self-control. The psychological burden became much greater, for Catholicism had included a 'safety-valve' which Calvinism rejected. The Catholic Church preached that man should not sin, but recognizing man's frailty, fallibility, and inherently sinful nature, came to terms with the fact that man would inevitably sin: the institution of confession provided an accommodation for that fact. Calvinism, on the other hand, simply demanded that men should not sin, and made no allowance for the frailty of human nature. Calvinists must not sin, but should continually re-examine their conduct and their thoughts to eliminate every sinful deed and desire, in order to lead the life of the saint.[26]

One cultural consequence of the Christian emphasis on sin and the sense of guilt which its teaching induced was the extraordinary extent to which religion and morality became interlocked in western societies, at both the private and the public levels. Bad conduct had implications not merely as the cause of supernaturally induced evil effects but as a direct affront to religious faiths. Further, such a negative act had the consequence—at least in the well-socialized individual who sought social esteem—of producing its own psychological reaction: an individual became fearful because he had transgressed against the will of God. Men were anxious about their behaviour not because each act had an unknown effect at some indeterminate future time, but because each wrongful act—acts in everyday economic and social intercourse as well as sacral or sexual offences—might be taken as a sign that one's soul was destined to perdition. For Christians, earthly life was a once-and-for-all opportunity to do God's will and to seek a blissful life

[26] For a recent attempt to widen the application of Freud's analysis of religion and culture (which does not, however, extend to religions of the Far East), see C. R. Badcock, *The Psychoanalysis of Culture*, Oxford: Blackwell, 1980.

eternal; it was not one of innumerable reincarnations, the misfortuntes and lost opportunities of which might be ascribed to bad karma inherited from the remote past, and for which the individual might console himself by remembering that there were future incarnations to come in which he might make better progress towards eventual enlightenment.

The privatization of responsibility in Puritanism, and in the pietistic and evangelical styles of Protestantism which followed in the eighteenth and nineteenth centuries, influenced the culture of some western countries most profoundly. The dependence on internalized control led men to acquire strong moralizing dispositions, and even though these operated informally they none the less came to characterize a particular cultural style, which was pronounced not only, as is often supposed, among the middle classes, but also among those considerable sections of the lower classes who counted themselves as 'respectable'. Public acts became the subject of moral scrutiny, and the private morals of public men became a recurrent concern in Protestant countries. In the period of religion's greatest vigour, living a life 'holier than thou' became a preoccupation, the informal keeping of each other's consciences became a characteristic of the Protestant societies of the West, and moral stricture became the characteristic mode of censure. The moral tolerance of Buddhist society, in both the Theravada and Mahayana traditions, stands in sharp contrast to the moral intolerance which often acquired political expression, and which for a long time was typical of Protestant cultures, in which public reputation and private, and particuarly, sexual, morality became strongly linked. Yet, in the longer run of history, we may doubt whether the intensity of the psychological sanction of guilt was more effective in inducing high standards of moral comportmnt, than the less rigorous conceptions linking action and responsibility in other religious traditions.

When, in the West, religion waned, when the rationalistic forces inherent in Puritanism acquired autonomy of their religious origins, so the sense of moral propriety also waned— albeit somewhat later, as a cultural lag. Following the decline of religion, although not explicitly and directly as a consequence of it, came a process of moral breakdown, and the so-called 'new morality' or 'permissive morality' was born. A philosopher could even announce a course of lectures a few years ago with the title, 'What *was* morality?'—an indication that he perceived the end of a moral era.[27] The emphasis on 'doing your own thing' was a further indication of the disappearance of social consensus about morals, first in ex-Protestant, and subsequently also in still nominally Catholic, societies. The links between religion and morality had been close, and the decline of religion appears necessarily to have brought about in its train a process of uncertainty about morals, and the abandonment both of earlier moralizing attitudes and the genuine concern about the role of morality in contemporary culture. In consequence, the socialization of children has become an intensely problematic issue in contemporary societies. Without the reinforcement of religious apprehensisons, moral guidance by teachers, or even by parents, has become difficult to provide. Consensus has gone, and the assumption of public support for a distinctive moral code has disappeared. In societies in which religion has not so directly provided specific injunctions for moral behaviour, the consequence of this breakdown may be avoided—unless eastern nations simply imitate the range of morally permissive behaviour now evident in the West.

Of the innumerable differences in the cultures of different societies, not all. are attributable to the specific influence of religion, and yet most sociologists have had little doubt about the determining power of religious ideas, practices, and attitudes in the moulding of societies in the past. Understandably, more attention has been paid to western societies—the culture within which sociology itself first developed—but the way is now open for further detached and objective studies into the role of religious ideas, practices, and institutions in their influence on the social organization and development of other societies. Those studies should be undertaken before the most powerful current at work in this sphere today, namely the process of secularization, erodes distinctive religious differences in various cultures. Today, the religious inheritance of many societies is increasingly disavowed, the religious view of the world is replaced by the intimations of science and technoogy,

---

[27] The philosopher, then at Oxford University, was Alasdair MacIntyre. For a critique of the permissive morality from a philosophical perspective, see C. H. and W. M. Whiteley, *The Permissive Morality*, London: Methuen, 1964; and for an analysis of moral change, see Christie Davies, *Permissive Britain*, London, Pitman, 1975.

and the facets of social life that were forged by religion are radically altered. The process is in itself a threat to what men have meant by culture, to the constellation of artefacts, norms, values, attitudes, and collective mental constructs by which men in a given society mediate their relationships and order their affairs. The implications of science for values are perhaps bleak, and the increasingly rationalized world order is one in which cultural distinctiveness may well be eliminated, not only for social classes, ethnic groups, regions, and age-strata, but even also for entire societies. It is difficult for me to believe that there will be any political or economic gains that will in any way compensate for the loss of cultural richness and diversity and the unique manifestations of the human spirit, if any such development comes to pass.

At present, in the West, the remnants of religion are, if receding, as yet still in evidence, but generally it may be said that western culture lives off the borrowed capital of its religious past. It is by no means clear what sort of society is coming into being as religious values wane. The consequences, not only for the arts and for high culture, but also, and perhaps more importantly, for the standards of civic order, social responsibility, and individual integrity, may be such that the future of western civilization itself may be thrown into jeopardy. To opine that these effects might ensue, is not, of course, to imply that the particular religious values of western society were in any sense either intrinsically warranted or specifically necessary for the maintenance of civilized order. It is, rather, to suggest that at least in western society the functions that were in the past supplied by, or at least supported by, religion, may now be left unserviced, and so to raise the question of whether in the future the conditions of life will ever be wholly humane without the operation of some such agencies.

4

The Sociology of Sects

The concept of the 'sect' has a very distinctive history. In English, it is a term that designates a religiously separated group, but in its historical usage in Christendom it carried a distinctly pejorative connotation. A sect was a movement committed to heretical belief and often to ritual acts and practices that departed from orthodox religious procedures. In practice, the Christian sect often rejected the liturgical cere-monial of the churches, and it declared itself competent without the services of priests (who claimed to have a monopoly of legitimate religious functioning as intermediaries between God and men). The term acquired its currency in sociology from the writings of Ernst Troeltsch, the German theologian and sociologist, who sought to characterize the distinction within Christianity of two types of radically opposed organizational forms—the Church and the sect.[1] As a model of the Church, Troeltsch had in mind the established churches as they were found in the nation state of his own times, and particularly the Evangelical Church in Germany, but he also intended his analysis to apply to the Catholic Church, which could, of course, claim a greater measure of universality than prevailed among the Protestant national churches.

Typology and religious change
The contrast of *church* and *sect* is at once historically confining and religiously specific. Troeltsch represented the contrast as a series of dichotomous variables by the use of which he could

[1] The original discussion will be found in Ernst Troeltsch, *Die Soziallehren der christlichen Kirchen und Gruppen*, Tübingen: Mohr, 1912 (trans. O. Wyon., *The Social Teaching of the Christian Churches* New York: Macmillan, 1931, 2 vols.) For a Roman Catholic objection to the Troeltschean formulation, see the partisan discussion by Werner Stark, *The Sociology of Religion: A Study of Chrstendom*, vol. III, *The Universal Church*, London: Routledge 1967, esp. pp. 95–6.

present in high relief the distinctive characteristics of each type of religious organization. He did not suggest, of course, that the terms had any application outside the community of Christian religious movements, and his own analysis was historically limited and relatively specific. Although Troeltsch disregarded the pejorative connotations which the term *sect* normally conveyed in popular discourse, and although subsequent sociologists have employed this concept in a strictly neutral sense, none the less, in everyday speech, the term retains the implication of disparagement.

If this difficulty were the only one involved in using the concept it might be ignored. But the term must also be divested of some of the implications that it acquired from its theological origins, and from its use outside the contexts of sociological discussion. In particular, it becomes evident in pluralist societies, such as advanced countries now exemplify, that the values of contrasting *church* and *sect*—even in countries in which a Christian church is 'established' (in the sense of enjoying distinct legal privileges over other religions)—has considerably diminished; this exercise of comparison may now be regarded as more of a hindrance to sociological analysis than a help. This is so because sects, today, do not normally arise in schisms from established churches, nor do they usually arise in specific protest against the Church. The generality of church-goers in western countries are not deeply committed religious people. Church-going is often conventional and, in some respects, and more especially so in America than in Europe, the content of church services and religious worship has become itself considerably diluted. There has been a process of internal secularization within the churches, which may be seen in the prevailing confusion about doctrines, in the persisting uncertainty about liturgy, in indifference to ecclesiology, and in the widespread open challenge to religious authority at many points. The likelihood that sects arise among churchgoers who break away in schism from their church over specific matters of belief, practice, appeals to legitimacy, or authority is now relatively slender. In general, sects arise among those who are outside the churches, or at least arise without so much direct relevance to church involvement, and although the members of a sect are generally much more committed to their specific beliefs than are the members of churches, there need be no specific relationship between these two types of organization or the people who belong to them.

Although the old relationship between church and sect no longer obtains, and although the dichotomous variables with which Troeltsch sought to characterize these two types of religious organization no longer hold in their entirety, it is the decay of the church-type of organization that has caused this change. Paradoxically, and using the term in a broader and looser sense, sects are now more universal than churches; separated groups of religious believers are now much more widespread, but they no longer take the church as the point of reference for their own self-definition. However, the basic characteristics of sects, as Troeltsch enunciated them, and as subsequent sociologists have refined them, may be said, in general, still to be relevant to a sociological understanding of these movements, and are worth repeating.

As recognized in Christian cases, sects manifest a variety of characteristics. (1) They tend to be exclusive, in the sense that they do not admit of dual allegiances: a sectarian is committed to only one body of religious teaching, and has only one membership. (2) Sects tend to claim that they have a monopoly of the complete religious truth, which others do not enjoy. This truth provides the framework for all aspects of belief, religious worship, social practice, ethics, politics, and all areas of human affairs; it may also embrace an understanding of the natural world, and the purposes and order that are thought to underlie the universe. (3) Sects also tend to be lay organizations. They may develop a body of professional functionaries and organizers, but they are generally anti-sacerdotal. This is implicit in the assumption that is made by sectarians that all men have some equal possibility of access to the truth. That such an assumption should so often be apparent in the operation of sects arises from the need of the inspirators of these movements to legitimize their own departure from prevailing orthodoxy—an orthodoxy warranted and sustained by the claims of a priestly class. (4) As far as specifically religious practice goes, sects tend to reject the religious division of labour, and to deny special religious virtuosity to anyone, except, in some cases, to their own founders and leaders. Religious obligations are equal obligations for all 'those who accept the truth' (as sects frequently define their own members). (5) It is thus implicit that sects are marked by voluntarism. An individual chooses to be a sectarian, and he is normally required to show some mark of merit (by knowledge of doctrine; quality of life; the recomendation of members in good standing; initiations or ritual performances, and so on) in order to be accepted as a member. (6) In conformity with this last requirement, sects exercise concern for sustained standards among their members, and it is usually the case that they exercise sanctions against the inadequate or wayward, to the point of expelling such individuals from the sect. (7) Sects tend to demand total allegiance. The member of any of the conventional churches in western countries may not appear in his everyday life to be very different from other religiously-uncommitted, or completely secular, men in his life-style, morals, interest, and leisure-time pursuits. This is not true of the sectarian—he is marked emphatically by his religious allegiance, which is expected to be evident in its influence on all areas of his life. The fact that a man is a member of such-and-such a group—a Mormon, a Seventh-day Adventist, or one of Jehovah's Witnesses—is in itself the single most important fact about him, telling one more of what to expect of him than any other piece of information pertaining to him.

(8) Finally, the sect is a protest group. And here it is the direction of protest tht has changed with the weakening of the dichotomous relation of church and sect. At one time, and no doubt in the European Middle Ages, the sect was a protest first and foremost against the Church, its teachings, and its priests. In the weakened condition of the contemporary Church, and in the tolerant, pluralist societies of the modern industrial western world, the Church no longer constitutes a significant object of protest. If the sect is still a protest group—and I think there is strong reason to suggest that it is—then it is a group that is in protest not against other religious bodies, but against the secular society, and, in some measure, possibly also against the state. The sect asserts a standard of religious practice and performance which has implications for personal comportment, for interpersonal relationships and responsibilities, and for social involvement (although this will not always, nor perhaps even usually, be expressed in directly political terms). Its 'charter' stipulates an interpretation of the higher purposes that are to be discovered in life, and perhaps in the universe, and, in

accordance with these, the sect directs men about how they should live. It is implicit in these affirmations that there must be divergences from, and perhaps outright conflicts with, the precepts of the secular society, and at times with the requirements of the state. The sect, then, remains a protest group, although what it protests about is much more the social, cultural, and political condition of the world than the specifically religious dispositions of other people or the power and the postures of the church.

These features of sectarianism have been taken by sociologists both to make apparent the elements that typically distinguish the sect from other types of religious organization—churches and denominations—and also to bring out into higher relief the fundamental dispositions of sectarianism. The development of pluralistic societies has the effect of making sects somewhat less distinctive in certain respects, and at least as *a type of organization*, since voluntary commitment increasingly becomes the hallmark of all religious movements. In the modern state, the churches, too, tend to become denominationalized, as they lose their claim to special status, and as orthodox religious commitment weakens. Voluntarism becomes the norm in religion—as in other departments of life—and established churches, which long ago lost their power to coerce, have increasingly lost even the force of conventional influence over the masses of the population, just as they have been forced to abandon the position of mutual reinforcement that they once enjoyed with the agencies of the secular state. To all this, we add the force of secularization, which has meant a loss of power for conventional religion, but which has in itself not affected sects to anything like the same extent, and, indeed, we have already noticed that it is the secular culture that becomes the focus of a considerable part of sectarian proest. We may even expect that, whereas in conditions of accelerating secularization, the churches lose support and influence, in precisely the same circumstances new sects emerge and flourish in specific rejection of the secular.

However, not all aspects of contemporary culture are entirely out of accord with the principles that sectarianism has generally espoused. The fact that authority is, in the modern world, under more explicit attack, and that old authority structures are discredited, makes sectarian protest appear much less exceptional. Thus, for example, the claims of the priesthood in Christian churches are now very much less emphatically made than once they were. Sacerdotalism is much less vigorously proclaimed, and even within the Roman Catholic Church, there are now voices—mainly those of theologians—which seek to reduce the distinctions between priests and laymen, even to the point of alleging that such distinctions were illicitly created by the Church in the past.[2] Belatedly, the Roman Church has learned the lessons of Protestantism, and church liturgy, hierarchy, and priestly authority are in the process of accommodating to much more demotic patterns of worship. In the Anglican Church, doctrinal formulations, about which fierce persecution occurred three centuries ago, are now abandoned for propositions that are much nearer to the stance that some sectarians long ago adopted. At least in these respects, then, sectarians are, today, apparently relatively less extreme than once they were. They are, of course, characterized by some distinctive teachings and practices in the case of each particular movement, but what perhaps most of all distinguishes them from other men is the intensity of their commitment.

In the matter of moral values, however, sectarian teaching is by no means always fundamentally different in kind from the traditional moral orientations of orthodox Christianity.[3] But the sects are more intense, more scrupulous, and more demanding about their moral requirements. Frequently, they emphasize the traditional virtues always canvassed in the Christian faith, but they do so with very much more effect on their believers than is the case with the churches, and they demand a much higher standard of ethical performance. Some sects have, of course, arisen specifically from deliberate campaigns aimed at the 'revival' of commitment. Their intensity alone has sometimes been enough to distinguish them from more conventional denominations, the members of which,

[2] The Constitution of the Roman Church, as established at the 2nd Vatican Council, no longer confines the concept of priesthood to a distinct class, but acknowledges the priesthood to be the possession of 'the faithful'. For more outspoken and more radical views, see, for example, Hans Küng, *Why Priests?* London: Collins Fontana, 1972; and Hervé Legrand O.P., in *Pro Mundi Vita*, 'New Forms of Ministries in Christian Communities', 50 (1974). See also Joseph A. Jungmann, *The Mass of the Roman Rite*, New York: Benziger, 1959.

[3] The point was long ago recognized by Benton Johnson, 'Do Holiness Sects socialize in dominant values?' *Social Forces*, 39, 4 (1961), pp. 309–16. The case might be illustrated from other sects besides those that might be described as holiness movements.

in sectarian eyes, appear to have become lax and to have compromised with the world. Since sectarians manifest their commitment in everyday life, it is largely in their moral comportment that their distinctive religious orientations are made evident, and often there is a strong feeling that it is in their lives that sectarians must prove to others that they are a separate people with an elevated morality. Thus we may say that some sects represent a powerful return to what they regard as having been the pristine message of the faith, in response to which they call for a new level of dedication and performance. This circumstance is most particularly in evidence in the early burgeoning of a particular movement.

Ideal-type analysis and sect dynamics

What has already been outlined as the characteristics of sects represents what sociologists call an 'ideal type'.[4] That is to say, the elements we have specified—exclusivity; total commitment; protest orientation; voluntarism; accession by merit; and so on—are formulated as expectable features of sects. They are set out as an extended definition in which are shown the logically coherent elements of a structure. It must be clear, that a given empirical example of what we recognize as a sect may, in fact, conform to only some of these expectations. For specific historical reasons, or because of arbitrary or adventitious circumstances, a movement that we generally acknowledge as a sect may depart in various particulars from this ideal-typical representation of 'the sect'. The ideal type is constructed in the full knowledge that actual cases diverge from it, and indeed it is precisely such a discrepancy between the ideal type and empirical cases which is useful, since it indicates just what it is that the sociologist should now seek to explain in a given empirical case. If all sects conformed completely to the constructed ideal type we should already know, on the evidence that allowed us to construct the ideal type itself, enough to 'explain' each individual sect. On the other hand, the ideal type must in its logical coherence be close enough to empirical cases to stand as a plausible, and indeed convincing, set of

---

[4] On ideal types, see Max Weber, *The Methodology of the Social Sciences*, (trans. E. Shils and H. A. Finch), Glencoe, Ill.: The Free Press, 1949. A more extensive discussion is provided by John C. McKinney, *Constructive Typology and Social Theory*, New York: Appleton Century Crofts, 1966.

generalized specifications of the phenomena. Reality does not conform to ideal-typical patterns, and the value of constructing ideal types is to provide a stable definition: the type is a measuring rod against which to examine actual empirical cases. It is a 'sensitizing' instrument, alerting us to the distinctive features of particular sects that stand in need of sociological and historical investigation.

Troeltsch, following the analysis promoted by Max Weber, produced the first general ideal-type formulation of 'the sect'. But Troeltsch's empirical evidence—the material from which he built up his formal typology—was very much coloured by the historical evidence of European mediaeval sectarianism, with which he was so well acquainted. Not only was the actual concept of the sect affected by its distinctively Christian origins, and by the specific historical and cultural conditions in which it was produced, but Troeltsch was not well acquainted with the sectarianism of his own times, as it was manifested either in Germany or, more particularly, in the Anglo-Saxon countries. In some respects, as cultural conditions had changed—and we have already noted some of these circumstances—so had the character of sects and their relationship to the wider society. It might, therefore, be said that one incidental effect of ideal-type constructs—when used indiscriminately—might be to create a false sense of timelessness and a historicity of particular concepts, and so of the phenomena which they define. We may see such another example of the tendency, even though his use of ideal types was less systematic, in the influential work of H. Richard Niebuhr.[5] He made a number of profound observations of some aspects of contemporary sectarianism of the late nineteenth and early twentieth centuries in America. But Niebuhr tended to assume that what he observed of some sects was true of all of them, and in particular he formulated a proposition, which clearly had some plausibility in the American context of the period, that sects became denominations in the course of one generation.

What Niebuhr observed was that sects began as radical

    [5] H. Richard Niebuhr, *The Social Sources of Denominationalism*, New York: Holt, 1929. This work is the departure point for an extensive literature on the development of sects into denominations; among other studies, see especially Liston Pope, *Millhands and Preachers*, New Haven: Yale University Press, 1942, pp. 118ff.

protest groups, but that over time they became more concerned with training the second generation than with the activities of proselytizing and converting outsiders. Their attempt to socialize the young children of existing members led them to acquire increasing concern with education, and this involved them in a range of more secular commitments, including the acquisition and management of property, and often a tendency to seek, and acquire, increased social respectability. Not infrequently, in the second generation, sects had also become relatively prosperous, and members sought status congruity with their personal wealth, so influencing their movement to take on styles of increased worldly respectability. The process which Niebuhr observed, and which he termed 'denominationalization', might in part also be described as 'institutionalization', at least in so far as it implied not only the relaxation of stringency in moral attitudes, and increased openness to other movements, but also, very often, increased formalism, including both more ritualistic styles of worship and the development of permanent officials in replacement of the initial spontaneity that had characterized the sect.

Niebuhr appeared to believe that he had discovered a universal law relating to sects—or at least, he expressed his thesis in terms of considerable generality. In comparison with its original intensity, sectarian protest, he contended, steadily became attenuated. Increasingly, sects became more tolerant of other religious movements, and gradually they came to allow that other movements might also offer valid ways to salvation: the sect gradually ceased to claim a monopoly of religious truth. The leaders increasingly became aware of the secular world, and came increasingly to accommodate secular assumptions in their organization, their moral pronouncements, and in their self-presentation. The early vigorous enthusiasm was now embarrassing, and became tempered by more sedate and sophisticated attitudes.

Much as his analysis facilitated the general understanding of sect development, Niebuhr had, in fact, rather over-generalized his observations. What eventually became apparent was that not all sects in Christendom followed the same course of development. In particular, some groups managed to retain a distinct sectarian stance in face of the wider society, whilst others changed in the ways (or some of the ways) that Niebuhr had hypothesized.[6] Ideal-type analysis was the means by which the attempt was made to distinguish just which sects might develop in the direction of becoming a denomination—that is, a tolerant, world-accommodating religious movement that had abandoned most, if not all, of the distinguishing features of sectarianism—and which would persist as sects in the strict sense of the term. It became apparent, from such analysis, that there were several distinctive styles of sectarianism, and that only certain types of sect, manifesting particular features, were likely to become denominationalized in the way that Niebuhr had predicted.[7]

In particular, sects that came into being as intense reaffirmations of an older religious tradition that was no longer being maintained in it pristine rigour were precisely those which were themselves most likely, in the course of time, to undergo a similar process of denominationalism to that of the old movement out of which they stemmed and which they sought to revive. These sects, which often began in revival campaigns in which the old-time faith was reaffirmed with emotional intensity, often began as rebukes to conventional Christians who were impugned for their failure to take their faith sufficiently earnestly. But these new movements tended to recruit at mass revival meetings, and often they came into existence more on a wave of emotionalism than on solid doctrinal or liturgical experience, or even as a result of long-sustained ethical concern and commitment. The people drawn into these sects remained in need of guidance in their religious lives and with respect to their moral comportment, and so it was that these sects tended, from quite early in their development, to need the services of religious specialists—that is to say, of a ministry of full-time counsellors and pastors. Such a development amounted to the creation of an incipient religious division of labour, which implied, from even quite an early stage, the attitudes of dependency on the part of the laity, and led an increasingly sophisticated ministry to become more and more embarrassed about excessive emotional expressiveness. Over time, the tendency of the ministry was to reduce worship

---

[6] The concept of the established sect developed by J. Milton Yinger, *Religion, Society and the Individual*, New York: Macmillan, 1957, pp. 151–2, clearly disputed Niebuhr's generalizations.

[7] This analysis was originally developed by B. R. Wilson, 'An Analysis of Sect Development', *American Sociological Review*, 24, 1, (1959) pp. 3–15.

activity to more prosaic ritualized patterns, to become concerned about socialization, and to some extent with their own
status, and particularly with the comparison between themselves and the ministries of other movements, who became an
increasingly relevant reference group for them. All of these
tendencies led to a more denominational position in the course
of time.

A process similar to that outlined in the foregoing paragraph
might easily be documented from the histories of a number of
Protestant religious movements, particularly in the United
States: they began in sectarian fervour but, in the course of
sometimes only two or three decades, they had acquired all the
respectability and the concern for status typical of the socially
well-adjusted and socially-accommodating denomination.[8]
There were specific cultural and historical reasons for the
frequency of this process of development. In particular, the
dynamic growth of American society was generated by
recurrent waves of immigration, which brought in new,
uneducated and socially disprivileged groups, who formed a
new bottom stratum of the class structure and from among
which new, emotional religions of the disinherited and socially
anomic groups recurrently recruited. For each growth there was
a relatively rapid process of social mobility, and as each group
rose in the scale, as other migrants arrived behind, and
necessarily below, them, so its religious expression lost its initial
fervour and acquired additional respectability and status. It
was such movements which Niebuhr observed, and from his
observation he built a theory of sect development which
depended on the particular, historically and culturally unique,
circumstances of the United States in the late nineteenth and
early twentieth centuries.

Since, in other periods and in other cultures, other sects could
be shown to have developed in quite different ways from that
postulated in Niebuhr's thesis, it became a matter of sociological
importance to find a basis for distinguishing among sects.
Recourse was again had to ideal-type constructs, which were
used to provide more refined explanations of sect emergence and

---

[8] For two examples, see E. D. C. Brewer, 'Sect and Church in Methodism', *Social
Forces*, 30, (1952), pp. 400–8; and O. R. Whitley, 'The Sect to Denomination Process in
an American Religious Movement, The Disciples of Christ', *Southwestern Social Science
Quarterly*, 36 (1955), pp. 275–82, and idem, *The Trumpet Call of Reformation*, St. Louis:
Bethany Press, 1959.

persistence, and more precise predictions concerning the probable course of development of particular sects: in short, what was now sought was a comparative theory of sectarianism.[9] A number of more rigorous ideal-type constructs were developed which sought to distinguish among sects with respect to their basic orientations and the likelihood of particular sequences of sect evolution. This analysis appears to have been useful and successful with respect to the interpretation of Christian sectarianism. (That application should first have been made to cases of Christian sects is understandable, given that both sociology generally, and the sociology of religion in particular, were first developed by scholars whose background and culture was Christian; those disciplines have remained most fully developed in countries with a tradition of Christian culture.) The analytical apparatus, briefly described, constituted a typology of seven types of sect, each characterized by its own self-declared mission in the world, which was later and more aptly designated as the sect's 'response to the world'. All of these seven sub-typifications of the sect conformed to the broader ideal-type construct of the sect taken as a generic type, as we have outlined it above, but, to this general characterization were now added specific elements which comprised each of the seven distinctive responses to the world.

Biases and limitations
The sub-types were elaborated with respect to specific variations that might arise within the context of the Christian tradition, but it was not immediately clear just to what extent the typology as a whole implicitly depended on assumptions that were peculiar to Christianity, or, alternatively, to what extent it was capable of wider application beyond the confines of one cultural and religious tradition. In general, it may be said that sociologists have a strong wish to establish categories and concepts that have as wide an application as possible. Indeed, it has been characteristic of sociological theory—perhaps influenced in this respect by the model afforded by theoretical physics—that its concepts should be valid for a spaceless and

[9] B. R. Wilson, op. cit. The typology developed in this article was extended later; see B. R. Wilson, 'A Typology of Sects', in *Types, Dimensions et Mesure de la Religiosité*, Actes de la X Conference Internationale de Sociologie Religieuse (Rome 1969), pp. 29–56; idem, *Religious Sects*, London: Weidenfeld, 1970 (Tokyo, Heibonsha, 1973); and idem, *Magic and the Millennium*, London: Heinemann, 1973, pp. 18–30.

timeless social universe, without regard to cultural specificity or historical contingency, as if geography and history had no relevance for theoretical models and constructs. Yet, it is clear that such a high degree of generalization might be possible only if the sociologists' concepts were developed to a very high level of abstraction. Unfortunately, as anyone who has engaged in empirical sociological enquiry knows, concepts at a high level of generality and abstraction are often of very limited value in application to any one specific culture.[10] They may provide a basis for far-reaching comparisons, but they do not come very close to the specifics of any given case, and they do little help us grapple with empirical evidence.

The ideal-type construct of the sect proved, in practice, to lack the generality that might have been expected of it. Although it had something of the appearance of a conceptual apparatus of considerable generality and abstractness, there were, in fact, concealed within it elements that depend on the specific assumptions of the Christian tradition. Certainly, the term 'sect' was widely employed, both popularly and sociologically, to designate the separate and distinct religious movements within the compass of other broad religious traditions, but many of the fundamental features that were implicitly assumed in the concept derived essentially from the evidence of Christian sectarianism, and these are not legitimate assumptions for other, non-Christian, cases. Ideal types are themselves produced only after the theorist has acquired a very considerable knowledge of the empirical evidence pertinent to his study. The ideal-type constructs represented logical coherent patterns of sectarianism, but these patterns were themselves in part dependent on a type of logic that was present in the Christian tradition, but which was by no means always evident, explicitly or implicitly, in other religious cultures.

To take an obvious example: the logic of the ideal type of the sect explicitly requires that members will not be permitted to maintain any commitment to other religious movements; the Christian sect requires exclusivity of commitment. But the groups of 'separated' religionists in other cultures by no means always maintain an exclusivist position. In many parts of the

[10] The point is explicitly made by Max Weber, whose work was largely responsible for a more conceptual and abstract approach to social phenomena; see *The Methodology of the Social Sciences*, op. cit., p. 80.

world, indeed, dual or multiple religious allegiance is not uncommon. Such multiple allegiance seriously modifies the essentials of the concept of the sect as it has developed in western (Christian) society, in which a principle of non-contradiction is strongly maintained. Thus, as set forth in the ideal-type construct, the concept of the sect is usable in other cultures only with considerable circumspection.

Another problem which the sociologist who studies sects beyond the confines of the specifically western context may encounter arises from the fact that, as generally applied, the term 'sect' suggests particular patterns of organization, in which there is voluntary commitment on the part of the individual believers. Those who belong support a group which, even though in some cases it may give the impression of being no more than a socially separated community, is, in fact, a voluntary, consciously organized movement. Sects, as the term is understood in western societies, are always characterized by a consciously-sustained and deliberately instituted structure and pattern of order. Even groups that are long-settled and that give all the appearance of maintaining an unsophisticated communal life, such as is the case with the Amish Mennonites and the Hutterian Brethren, are in reality sustained in their separateness by agencies and officials who operate a selfconsciously applied pattern of organization. They have not only rules but codes and principles.[11] These communitarian groups have a structure that was deliberately instituted and amended, even though they have incorporated many incidental cultural features into what appears like a distinctive, almost ethnically determined way of life, none the less, there is always a basis of formal organization. At the other extreme, sects are not simply spontaneous collectivities. We should deny the term 'sect' to the initial outburst of spontaneous collective religious behaviour, no matter how distinctive such behaviour might be. The word would be reserved until such a movement had acquired some institutionalized procedures. Thus, there is always a principle of sustained, voluntary commitment, whether, on the one hand, the movement appears like an almost

---

[11] On the Amish Mennonites, see John A. Hostetler, *Amish Society*, Baltimore: Johns Hopkins University Press, 1963; and on the Hutterites, John W. Bennett, *Hutterian Brethren*, Stanford: Stanford University Press, 1967, and John A. Hostetler, *Hutterite Society*, Baltimore; Johns Hopkins University Press, 1974.

hereditary caste into which members are almost all inborn, as with the Amish; or, on the other, they appear to be only fleetingly involved.

In non-western cultures, however, movements that are called 'sects' sometimes appear to lack this element of conscious maintenance of a separate organization. Some of these groups— for example in Hinduism and Islam—are more like traditional ethnic groups that have long had an unself-conscious natural sense of community that requires no deliberate organizational underpinning. In consequence, to refer to these groups as 'sects', as if they conformed in their essentials to the model devised for the separated groups within western Christianity, would be to proceed on highly questionable assumptions and to risk a distorted sociological analysis.

The implications of the culture-bounded character of the ideal-type construct of the sect was borne in upon me when I attempted to use this mode of analysis (an analysis which I had had some part in developing) in the study of movements outside the Christian context and outside western culture.[12] In that endeavour, I found it necessary to abandon the rigorous application of sub-types of sect in favour of 'responses to the world', since this type construct did not carry with it the demand for, for example, either exclusivity or the particular assumptions about organization that are built into the concept of the sect as such. It was possible to distinguish among a wide variety of movements with respect to their own conception of evil and the way in which evil was to be surmounted, without postulating all the various specific characteristics that are true for Christian sects. My particular concern was to indicate the cultural conditions in which each of these responses (or orientations) was likely to arise, and to discover something about the social and cultural consequences that followed their adoption.

These discoveries—and social science is often a matter of discovering the limitations of analysis as well as discovering its further application—have acquired a new significance even for the study of sectarianism in contemporary advanced industrial societies, however. In recent years, the area of religious choice has broadened very considerably in the West: since the early 1960s, western countries have experienced the dramatic impact

[12] See B. R. Wilson, *Magic and the Millennium*, op. cit.

of movements that are loosely called 'sects', even though what is meant by the word is nothing more specific than that these religious movements obviously differ in a fundamental way from the indigenous Christian tradition of western society. (It is perhaps an interesting paradox that societies which, in the days of their greatest relative strength, devoted so much energy, time, and money to exporting Christianity to the rest of the world, should now become importers of a diverse array of the religious ideas and practices of older cultures.) These new movements may not always be adequately designated as 'sects', but in the context of western cultures they are popularly so-called because the recency and stridency of their non-European provenance readily distinguishes them from what appears normal religion. Some of these movements cultivate distinctive styles of dress, or pursue activities that make them socially conspicuous (such as selling literature or chanting in the streets, for example). Some of them undoubtedly seek the total allegiance of their adherents, even, in certain cases, to the point of seeking to establish entirely self-contained and separated communities. Yet these distinguishing features—life-style, communality, total commitment, and exclusivity—are not characteristic of all of them, and they do not all conform to the basic features of the ideal type of the sect as it has been developed in sociology. An important theoretical question arises at this point: namely, the extent to which an ideal type and given empirical cases may legitimately diverge. Obviously there are discrepancies between every actual sect and the ideal type 'sect'. The point of type construction is to delineate a probable and expectable constellation of related features and logical relationships and sequences, and, by comparing the type with actual phenomena, to become aware of the issues that stand in need of explanation. All actual empirical cases diverge from the ideal type, but there must clearly be a limit to such divergence, a point beyond which the cases cannot usefully be analysed by using the type as the appropriate measuring rod, simply because the case is too discrepant. One might say, a point at which the case concerned cannot be appropriately called a 'sect', and thus cannot be usefully analysed in the terms we have carefully devised as being specifically appropriate for the analysis of sects. It is not possible to resolve the theoretical difficulty here; we may simply note that an ideal type may need to be constructed with some idea of what are the 'reserved' or 'entrenched' clauses in its constitution. In the particular case we are reviewing, we may concede that our existing ideal type of the sect may not be the most appropriate sensitizing device for the analysis of the new religious movements that have recently emerged in western societies.

The question of whether a particular movement may or may not properly be called a 'sect' is in itself of relatively little interest; the question that matters is the appropriate tools for analysis. Some recent study of religious movements appears to me to have missed the point about the use of ideal types.[13] They are essentially tools, and their purpose is not one of classification. Type-constructs are *not* intended simply to allow us to designate classes of phenomena: they are to indicate, as we have said, the expectable logic of the social arrangements of a given genus of phenomena. It is a futile occupation to spend time on deciding whether a particular movement should be called a 'sect' or not. Ideal types are not empty boxes into which the sociologist drops appropriate cases; they are, rather, to be used to make us aware of the specific historical, organizational, compositional, or other features of a sect that depart from our hypothetical system of logical relationships. The type should always turn us back to historical or empirical data so that we can explain those features of a case that contradict our hypothesized common-sense assumptions.

Tradition and modernity in sectarianism
It is a characteristic of sects arising within a traditional culture that they are simultaneously both radical and conservative. They are radical in the challenge that they pose to constituted religious authority: they reject the procedures and activities of the dominant church, which they regard as invalid if not as perverted; they dissociate themselves from many aspects of secular culture; and they condemn at least those enactments of the state that they see as contravening the demands of true religion. On the other hand, they are conservative in that they often seek to re-assert moral and religious precepts which they see as having become neglected in the dominant tradition or in attempting to revive what they regard as uncorrupted religious performances, or an earlier pattern of organization which they

[13] For example. Geoffrey Nelson, *Spiritualism and Society*, London: Routledge 1969.

believe to have been divinely warranted. They condemn contemporary authority either for failing to maintain original religious ideals, or sometimes for falling to accept new revelation. Thus, they are radical in opposing the hierarchy of the dominant religious tradition, but conservative in proclaiming that there is an authority beyond that hierarchy which men should obey.

Sects in which radicalism and conservatism are mixed in some of these ways constitute the predominant form of sectarianism in western Christianity. Yet the need of each sect to establish a claim to legitimacy in practice restricts the range of possible postures that a sect may adopt. This is particularly so for those sects that seek to legitimize themselves by reference either to the Gospels or to the form of early Christian church organization. Even so, in any of a wide variety of matters that are not specifically laid down by the models of authority that they accept, a sect may adopt procedures that are in themselves radically new. Sects tend to be more influenced than they know or care to acknowledge by the prevailing secular facilities of the period of their emergence. Some sects quickly stabilize their life-practices in conformity with these prevailing techniques, and sanctify them to the point of refusing to permit any further change even in styles and arrangements that clearly have no specific religious significance, but which were simply secular styles at the time of the sect's formation. The Amish Mennonites, who originated in France, the Low Countries, and Switzerland, and who have retained their original peasant styles of clothes, recreations and work habits, despite their subsequent migration to the United States, are the most cogent example, and, in lesser measure, so are the Hutterites in Canada. These are, however, very old sects, locked in postures that were heavily conditioned by the time of their emergence or in some subsequent formative period. Other sects, of more recent provenance, or sects that have shown a remarkable adaptability in those matters not laid down by their original conception of their 'charter' (to use Malinowski's term) have managed to utilize contemporary techniques in association with ancient religious teachings.

The capacity to bring together ancient teaching and modern techniques is part of a formula of success for modern sects. It is in itself a sociologically interesting phenomenon because there is a tendency in religious movements towards institutionalism and conservatism. Patterns of organization, once adopted, tend to persist, as if they were in some sense legitimized and sanctified by ancient precepts, even though they were initially adopted purely as a matter of expediency. To take a conspicuous example: the Salvation Army adopted a military analogy for its operations, including uniforms, military terminology, and organizational styles, at its very beginning as a movement. The style was convenient at a time of militaristic enthusiasm, in a country that was then proud of its imperialism and its colonial adventures, and which had its soldiers scattered all over the world, even though its army was a totally voluntary (non-conscripted) army. The Salvation Army uniform attracted the poorer classes to which it made its appeal, since it conferred a measure of dignity and equality among the rank and file. The idea of an army suggested total commitment, obedience, self-sacrifice, heroism, and aggressive evangelism. The structure of authority within the movement was hierarchic on the military model. It was an authority structure of the type that was not only normal, but which was highly esteemed in the Britain of that age (the 1870s). The Salvation Army retains its style today, a hundred years later, even though the military analogy is no longer socially relevant, when imperialism is condemned, and the style of organization is very much out of favour with contemporary people with their anti-hierarchical attitudes. The uniform itself, and the procession and street services are all somehow out of date. Yet the form persists; the Salvation Army would not be itself without the maintenance of the military analogy, even though the 'brand image' that was once its best propaganda weapon is now probably a distinct handicap.[14]

The tendency for styles, techniques, and procedures to become sanctified, and to become associated with the sacred purposes of a movement, even though they were originally adopted merely as expedient choices, is not simply a consequence of man's conservatism. It is also a clear indication of the pervasiveness of a sense of the sacred and the tendency for religious dispositions to overspill their own specific areas of applicability. The forms become coloured by the content—the

[14] On the Salvation Army, see Roland Robertson, 'The Salvation Army: The Persistence of Sectarianism', in B. R. Wilson, *Patterns of Sectarianism*, London: Heinemann, 1967, pp. 49–105.

organization becomes an end in itself, not easily dissociated from the purposes that it was created to promote. The purely expedient becomes sanctified and legitimized in religious or quasi-religious terms. From a different perspective, it might be said that the purely organizational features of a movement become affected by the sense of sacredness because there is a powerful tension—certainly in western cultures—between the sacred and the profane. The profane aspects of a religious movement, such as its organizational structure, shall we say, or the territory and property that it occupies, need to become sacralized in order to prevent these essentially secular elements from tainting and secularizing the sacred. If they become sacralized, they reinforce the adherent's commitment by reducing the tension that otherwise might arise between the instrumental and organizational concerns and the substantive and arbitrary goals of the movement. The secular world is kept at bay by making even expedient matters into matters of religious principle and religious poetry.

Between specifically rational styles of operation and ultimate religious purposes there exists a particularly high measure of tension. Religions are organized to sustain certain particular, and in this sense, arbitrary, given and 'received' ideas, performances, objects, places, or events. These things have symbolic importance far beyond their intrinsic significance. Their meaning and purport cannot be reduced to terms of strict instrumental rationality. Ultimately, religion is always a matter of faith and deliberate commitment of the will, and it is always maintained that the exercise of faith transcends all empirical or pragmatic tests. Rational organization, in contrast, requires that the most efficient means be used to attain well-defined ends (which in themselves should not conflict with other ends). Rational procedures are specific, purposive, empirically validated, and pragmatically tested. The religious act is an end in itself, performed regardless of cost. The rational act is always an end within a chain of means-ends relationships, in which costs are narrowly calculated. There is, therefore, always a likelihood of tension between the religious and the rational.

In spite of these considerations, modern sects manifest an increasing capacity to utilize rational procedures for their ultimately religious ends. It would be surprising, given the increasingly rational structure of contemporary society, were this not so; indeed, it might be argued that sects have not infrequently stimulated the adoption of rational techniques and the development of rational attitudes. This has been the case, because sects are a radical challenge to tradition, which is a position from which they can easily adopt simple and rational techniques with which to make apparent the inadequacies of traditional approaches. The fact that this disposition to rationality affronts the religious susceptibilities of traditional religionists merely confirms in the minds of the orthodox their conviction that the sectarians are heretics who will destroy the true faith. The rationalistic orientation was, of course, evident in Puritanism, and again in Methodism, as their very adoption of that name suggests. They were determined to be methodical in their religious devotions, and they built up a rational organization to this end. In Christian Science, founded just over a century ago, the words *science* and *Christian* were conjoined to indicate the possibility of a rational interpretation of religion; that movement always made much of the idea that religion was a principle capable of rational and precise application. Christian Science adopted the styles and nomenclature of contemporary education to underscore the rational character of its doctrine, and developed courses and degrees as the appropriate means by which this religious truth was to be acquired. In recent years, the Church of Scientology has developed a similar system in which scientific procedures and religious ends are fused. It maintains an elaborate system of instruction, graded, set out, and scored in apparently rational order of increasing complexity. The movement teaches that men can attain heightened intelligence and emotional control by the practice of its therapeutic procedures, but these goals are themselves closely associated with the need for improved performances and achievement in the everyday sphere of work: the religious and the purportedly scientific again converge.

It is not, however, only those sects that are concerned with therapy that have adopted conspicuously rational patterns of organization. Even some movements with more fundamentalist and biblical orientation have adopted rational techniques and procedures for the dissemination of their message and the regulation of their processes of instruction. Sects as different from each other as Seventh-day Adventists, Christian Scientists, and Jehovah's Witnesses, utilize standard materials for study and worship in their services and meetings throughout the world.[15] The routinization of methods of proselytizing has been taken a very long way by the Witnesses, whose local leaders rigorously control the canvassing activities of the members of each congregation.[16] In every local meeting, there are leaders who are appointed to the specific task of training the members for the work of proselytizing and recruiting new converts. As these sects have become international bodies, so rational principles of organization have become indispensable to the maintenance of control and cohesion. These movements have grown up in societies that are themselves increasingly organized according to rational principles, and in consequence their membership readily accepts and adopts rational procedures which are normal in the wider society for their religious pursuits. Recruits may even feel attracted to the movement because of the conjunction of clear rational patterns of action with the distinctive teachings that are presented as matters of absolute truth commanding total obligation. There is no doubt that the institution of rational systems—in organization, missioning, financing, fund-raising, instructing, and conducting all operations that fall short of the actual sacred activities of worship—provides the most effective framework of control of the membership and the efficiency of function. And in some of these movements, activity that can be called worship or devotions is often very limited in time and scope (as in the cases of Christian Science, Scientology, and the Jehovah's Witnesses), which in itself enlarges the area in which the purely rational aspects of operation are manifested. Rational procedures ensure calculability and continuity of effort, reduce to a minimum the wayward or haphazard expression of unorthodox views, and provide effective co-operation and mutual control by participants one of another. Obviously, movements that rely heavily on rational precepts cannot also accommodate—except perhaps at the very top—inspirational or charismatic elements, nor facilitate very much spontaneity of expression or independent initiative except within the framework of established order.

[15] For a more extended discussion, see B. R. Wilson, 'American Religious Sects in Europe,' in C. W. E. Bigsby, (ed.) *Superculture: American Popular Culture and Europe*, London: Elek, 1975, pp. 107–22.

[16] For a detailed study of Jehovah's Witnesses, see James A. Beckford, *The Trumpet of Prophecy*, Oxford: Blackwell, 1975.

Alternative strategies for analysis

Despite the growing adoption of rational modes of operation among sects, contemporary sectarianism is perhaps more diverse in its teachings and orientations than have been the sects of the past, at least as sects are found within any one given cultural milieu. In large part, this follows from the new patterns of international exchange that has already been mentioned. Yet, despite the variety of actual movements, the sociologist must continue to look for common themes and common patterns among the many movements that operate. Whilst it is possible that the categories of 'response to the world', to which we have already referred, might provide some guidance to the analysis of these movements, equally some other ideal-typical formulations might prove to be more useful. It is important not to become too much attached even to an ideal-type formulation that has done good service in the past. One variation of the model of analysis by 'response to the world' that I developed in the past, would be to regard sects as manifesting diverse tendencies that we might label as world-denying, world-indifferent, and world-enhancing.[17] The world-denying sects would be those the teachings of which emphasize the evil of the modern world, which men must shun. In effect, they proclaim that men must be saved *from* the world. Such sects tend to draw their believers out into separate communes or collectivities, where a purer way of life is practised. World-indifferent sects tolerate the secular world whilst, as is implicit in the nature of sectarianism, they encourage their votaries to see a better way and a purer life within the world, attempting to be *in* the world whilst not being *of* the world. Their members associate predominantly with each other, whilst drawing short of seeking to establish a separate communal life: in economic activities, in particular, they might find themselves engaged in normal worldly activities, even if, in those activities they bring their own distinctive sectarian values to bear. The world-enhancing sect is a sect that self-consciously seeks to improve the skills and competences of its members so that they may, in general, enjoy life in the world more than they did hitherto, and find

---

[17] A distinction between 'world-affirming' and 'world-rejecting' sects was first developed by Roy Wallis, *The Rebirth of the Gods*, Inaugural Lecture, The Queen's University, Belfast, 1978, and is developed in Roy Wallis, 'The Elementary Forms of the New Religious Life', *Annual Review of the Social Sciences of Religious*, 3 (1979).

themselves a better place within it. The model of the world-denying sect is approximated, among recent movements, by the Children of God and the Krishna Consciousness movement. Some similarity to the ideal-typical construct of the world-indifferent sect might be found in various Pentecostal sects or in Jehovah's Witnesses (at least in their more recent history). Clearly, Christian Science, Scientology, and Transcendental Meditation most nearly meet the criteria of the world-enhancing sect.

Before such a framework for analysis is established, however, it is clearly essential to decide whether the intention is to create a set of ideal-type constructs that provide variant (and, ideally, exhaustive) constellations of values, or whether what is sought is merely a classificatory system. The scheme cursorily adumbrated here is at best suggestive of possibilities for analysis, but one must be aware that within any one sect there are almost always divergent strains, certainly evident over the course of time, and sometimes clearly discernible even at particular given points of time. Such discrepancies do not, of course, invalidate the ideal type constructs: indeed, within a certain compass, the type construct is used precisely to sensitize the analyst to such anomalies and ambiguities. But just how far a case may deviate from the type without impairing its utility (and ultimately even reducing the analysis to distortion by the application of a grossly inappropriate ideal-typical model) is a matter for judgement. Even to establish mere categories for classificatory purposes may be less easily done than at first sight appears, for sects are complex phenomena. Thus, a sect that teaches separation from the world may none the less inculcate moral precepts and values that facilitate an individual's worldly activities, and help him to success in them. Sects that embrace an element of communal living, as does the Unification Church, may none the less take up a distinctive political position which appears to endorse the *status quo* in capitalist nations. Internal diversity within a sect may be such that a movement may not always be quickly and unambiguously characterized.

There are, of course, other variables that might provide the basis for a system of categorization. There are groups that are intellectual and instrumental in their orientation—intellectual in the sense that emphasis is given especially to the business of acquiring a body of doctrinal knowledge, and instrumental in the sense of having well-defined empirical goals—often in the field of evangelism. On the other hand, there are sects that are essentially expressive, emotional, and consummatory, in which activity focusses on the opportunity to release tensions, to manifest emotional commitment in a context in which emotional indulgence is 'licensed' and legitimized by the group's own sense of appropriate worshipful attitudes. Some groups exist largely to provide this type of experience for their members, rather than for the acquisition of a specific body of doctrinal knowledge or to pursue specified empirical ends. Significant as they are, however, these broad distinctions can be no more than the departure point for the construction of an analytical apparatus. Since each sect presents a unique constellation of values and activities, the sociologist must eventually give specific and detailed attention to them. Ideal types—and much less classificatory categories—are not substitutes for historical and sociological investigation; they are not even a short cut to firm conclusions; and least of all are they devices by which the uninformed can catch truth by the forelock.

The social constituencies of sectarianism

Obviously, it is the social aspects of sects that concern the sociologist, and in particular some knowledge of the social composition of each movement may be regarded as basic to sociological understanding—so much so that historians have sometimes erred in supposing that the very term 'the sociology of sects' relates to nothing more than the social composition of these movements. Troeltsch tended to assume that sects arose among the poorer classes, who compensated for the deprivation in their lives by participation in the sectarian 'community of love'. This assumption is no longer an adequate approach to the study of sects—if, indeed, it ever was. Poverty is not the determinant of sectarianism. Sects have by no means generally been common in the poorest countries or regions of Europe, nor, within a given society, has it always been among the poorest sections that sects have arisen. By definition, sects are minority groups, but the poor have—at least until very recent times— generally been by far the largest part of a country's population. If sects do arise among the poor, they can at best embrace only a relatively small proportion of them. In actuality, of course, we also find sects among middle class groups, and many sects which successfully embrace within their membership people from very different social strata. Again, we may find between one cultural context and another, that a sect's composition varies: what is a poor sect in one society, or even in one region, may be constituted from a rather different spread of the population in some other context. This condition prevails among Jehovah's Witnesses, and among Seventh-day Adventists in various parts of the world.

The new sectarian movements in western countries, and particularly those that have originated in the East, or which purvey some variant of an eastern religious tradition, appear to have one distinctive feature which distinguishes them from at least most of the established sects of Christian history, and this is their conspicuous appeal to a specific generational group—the young. Following in the wake of the dissident sub-cultural development of the hippies, with their deviant, hedonistic life-style, these sects offered themselves as alternatives to the hippy sub-culture, and particularly to those who have become disenchanted with the deviant and delinquescent aspects of the 'hippy scene'. In part, these movements shared some continuity with elements in the hippy life-style, but in their demand for a disciplined commitment, they departed radically from it. Part of their appeal to young people lay in the fact that, coming newly from the East (or appearing to do so), they were untainted by association either with older age groups or with the censorious and interdictory attitudes of Christian sect-arianism. Nor did the fact that they were, in their own ways, equally concerned to elicit certain standards of performance and behaviour, and even to assert the demand for rigorous discipline destroy—indeed, it may even have enhanced—their appeal. In part, this may have occurred because these movements already had the strong image of being counter-cultural: the discipline which they enjoined was part of the way to some higher truth. It was not imposed because it served a wider social purpose; it was not identifiable in any way with the processes of social control within the wider society. The ethical precepts of these sects were not enjoined because they provided a training in some more elevated conception of citzenship, but as the way of a personal pilgrimage and as an expression of solidarity with the new community.

Age-groups as such are much less likely to provide stable constituencies for sects that are social classes, and it is probable that many of these movements have acquired a distinctly generational clientele which may not survive as a clientele as it grows older. Adherents may find, as they cease to be 'idealistic young people', that the communitarian life-style of some of these sects, or of the inner cadre within such a sect, is less congenial to them; and even where they are not involved in daily living with a sect they may none the less find that the ethical precepts that appealed to a particular generational age group are, later on, less adequate as the rules for life in the wider society. Nor can the communitarian sects be in any sense equated with the monastic orders of the past, even though some of them made strong appeal to young people at times. Those orders enjoyed the support of both the church at large, of which they were a part, and of the occupants of the secular roles of the wider society. New movements today do not enjoy this support, nor do they normally present their own activities as especially beneficial to society at large; indeed, many of them receive largely negative publicity from the mass media, and find themselves in periodic conflict with parents, school, medical authorities, or the police. Since they have given so much attention to a particular age group, some of these movements may fail to adjust to the need to respond to the changing interests and energies of an ageing clientele, and may indeed fail to make even psychic accommodation for their membership, or for the young children who are born to the members of the movement. We have yet to see whether these new movements can establish patterns of socialization for the culture of the second generation of converts or members.

The relative deprivation thesis

Among the fundamental issues of importance for the sociologist of sectarianism is the explanation of the emergence and appeal of particular sects at a given time and in a particular cultural milieu. The processes of conversion of individuals, and the way in which commitment is acquired and maintained, and transmitted to subsequent generations, are concerns of as much interest to the sociologist as they are to the leaders of the sects themselves, even if the approach to these matters is from quite a different position and is undertaken with quite different assumptions. Sociologists have put forward some general theories about the origins of religious groups, but these theories lack the rigour to be convincing in given cases. At best they are plausible approximations. Religion is frequently looked upon as a compensation, and the theory of relative deprivation has been used by some sociologists to explain the origins and development of sectarian religion in particular. What essentially the theory postulates is that within a given population there are individuals who experience a sense of relative deprivation, either because they have done less well in life than they expected, or because they have not succeeded as well as those in the reference group against which they choose to compare themselves. Put like this, deprivation appears to be primarily a matter of economic or status achievement, but more recent authors have emphasized the possibility that men may experience a felt sense of deprivation in other respects, for example in the matter of physical well-being, although there is little doubt that deprivation with regard to wealth, income, or status provides the most cogent cases.[18] The theory postulates that those who interpret their circumstances in this way are deceiving themselves either about the fact of deprivation or about its causes, or that they are frustrated because they cannot effect the basic conditions to which relative deprivation may be attributed. Were they to see these circumstances with complete objectivity—so the theory implies—then they would either accept their lot in life, or they would take strictly rational and practical action to effect changes. Since they have either a distorted view of the facts, or are completely deceived about the consequences or the causes of their present circumstances (as they appraise the situation in relation to that of others) so, it is argued, they turn to religion as a compensation.

The thesis is not entirely without plausibility, and little as it concedes to the normal claim by religionists—that they accept their particular beliefs solely because they are true—it must also be remembered that religion is sometimes offered explicitly as compensation. Christianity, for example, appeals to those who suffer or are heavily burdened to accept its saviour who promises relief and solace to precisely this class of people. Yet

---

[18] See Charles Y. Glock, 'The Role of Deprivation in the Origin and Evolution of Religious Groups', in Robert Lee and Martin E. Marty, (eds.) *Religion and Social Conflict*, New York: Oxford University Press, 1964, pp. 24–36.

this thesis does tend to make religion—and in particular the strongly-held, life-encompassing religiosity of the sects—into a dependent variable, and it implies that no one would hold such a view of the world were he not suffering, or deceived, or lacking in the capacity for sound cause-and-effect reasoning. Since a sect, by definition, is a minority religion, outsiders are more likely to find this type of assumption more convincing when applied to sects than when taken up with respect to majority religions, and more cogent when addressed to a sect other than that to which they themselves chance to belong. Clearly, special pleading of this kind can scarcely be admitted by sociologists.[19]

These are not the only objections to the relative deprivation thesis, however. A serious difficulty is that normally such deprivation can be identified only ex-post facto. Thus, those who have joined sects are assumed to have been deprived at some earlier time; the analyst then looks for evidence of deprivation in their background experience. However, it must be clear that many people may have experienced deprivation who have not joined religious movements, and others may have had a sense of deprivation (whether justified or not) and yet have resolved their problem in other ways. Beyond this, the thesis fails to explain the diversity of religious responses, although in some formulations the attempt has been made to suggest a relationship between types of relative deprivation (economic, social, physical, psychic or ethical) and specific forms of sectarianism. Yet, even with these distinctions, relative deprivation remains too gross a category to explain sect-arianism. It is rarely possible to produce independent evidence of the sense of deprivation, particularly since, even if individuals may be shown by objective criteria to have been deprived, this in itself is not evidence of a felt sense of deprivation. Alternatively, the thesis may posit that some people have felt relatively deprived subjectively, even when objective depriv-ation can be shown not to have existed; but to obtain evidence of these subjective states of mind is even more difficult. Further problems arise with respect to the way in which salient reference groups are chosen for the relative measurement by the

---

[19] For an attempt to widen the role of deprivation to explain religious dispositions among adherents of non-sectarian movements, see C. Y. Glock, B. B. Ringer, and E. R. Babbie, *To Comfort and to Challenge*, Berkeley and Los Angeles: University of California Press, 1967.

individual of his sense of deprivation. All these difficulties in testing the thesis leave it to be regarded as at best a plausible but untested, and perhaps untestable, hypothesis. Even were the various forms of evidence available, we must expect that there might be a wide variety of intervening circumstances between a felt sense of deprivation and induction into a sect. People in a particular circumstance of deprivation do not automatically encounter a form of sectarian expression that necessarily meets their needs. There are many steps between needs and their supply in the field of religious involvement. Nor need we suppose that the sense of deprivation is the only untoward condition against which sect allegiance might be a remedy.[20] Sects do fulfil other functions for their adherents.

Conversion and commitment

Sect membership is always a distinctive and intense commitment, and the sociologist must be interested in the way in which an individual is induced to accept the onerous demands that sect allegiance entails. For a complete understanding of the conversion process, individual cases must be examined.[21] Very broadly, we may hypothesize that a variety of conditions must be fulfilled for the individual to become a committed sect member. First, the particular sect must be available, operating within the particular social context. The individual must become aware of it and learn something of its activities and teachings. Clearly, this may happen in a number of ways: it may be introduced by canvassers, by relatives or friends, by seeing advertisements or being drawn into public meetings. But for the conversion to occur, he must have in his background experience that renders him in some measure sensitive to the message, the style, promises or prospects of the movement, or he must be attracted by the example of the members, by the appeal of association, or the atmosphere as he perceives it. Some of these elements may be intrinsic to the sect, others may, of course, be

[20] For a brief but cogent critique of the relative deprivation thesis, see Roy Wallis, *Salvation and Protest*, London: Francis Pinter, 1979, pp. 4–6.

[21] For a discussion of the conversion process to sectarianism, see L. Gerlach and V. Hine, *People, Power, Change*, Indianapolis: Bobbs Merrill 1970; James Beckford, 'Accounting for Conversion', *British Journal of Sociology*, XXIX, 2 (June 1978), pp. 249–62 and B. R. Wilson, 'Becoming a Sectarian: Motivation and Commitment', in Derek Baker (ed.) *Religious Motivation: Biographical and Sociological Problems for the Church Historian* (Studies in Church History, vol. 15), Oxford: Blackwell, 1978, pp. 481–506.

incidental or even extrinsic (such, for example, might be the influence of relatives). Some of the intrinsic attractions of a sect may be features that are common to a number of sectarian movements; others may be peculiar to one particular group.

Clearly, it is those intrinsic features that are most general to sects that can best be briefly enumerated here, although comparative studies should reveal the elements that are distinctive to particular movements. Of such general features, it is of course always the acceptance that a movement's teachings are uniquely true which is likely to be cited first as the basis for an individual's allegiance. But apart from this expected claim we may indicate the cumulative impact of a variety of common characteristics: the attention extended to a potential member; the care and concern that is manifested; the warmth and support of a strong community; the provision of meanings; the opportunity for expression (or even the possibility of learning a 'language' in which to express oneself); identification with a purpose wider than one's previous social involvements; the availability of answers to specific questions, and of activities that become a *raison d'etre* for living. Subsequently, the individual finds opportunities for status, for self-respect and for the occasions on which to command esteem; he becomes settled to a definite life-style which stands in sharp contrast with the normlessness and shapelessness of life in the wider society. He abandons competing activities, and restructures his inclinations and dispositions into conformity with, and reinforcement of, those of the sectarian group. He becomes insulated from the external order and acquires a new evaluation of it, and once the process is under way, social relationships within the community become the social context in which new values are constantly reiterated and reinforced. Conversion is a process of re-socialization to distinctive ideas and values. The convert learns a language and a life-style which become a part of himself as he takes on a new definition of his own individuality and personality and of the social collectivities in which he participates.

Clearly, to such a general scheme, each sect may contribute its own distinctive values, perhaps attracting certain person-ality types or—and this may be much the more important aspect—forging certain styles of personality. But sects are, it must be remembered, in a very high degree voluntary movements, and those who belong to them generally choose to commit themselves to this distinctive way of life. In the modern world, choice is widely available with respect to certain fundamental philosophical and religious orientations. In the advanced nations, in the free world, sects constitute perhaps the largest area of serious and unfettered voluntary commitment that individuals enjoy. The importance of these movements to modern society, and for an understanding of it by sociologists, lies in the fact that sects represent a more serious commitment than do any mass leisure activities. They are more emphatically voluntary organizations than are trades unions, membership of which is often obligatory. They offer a wider range of possibilities and more abiding and more penetrating commitment than do political parties. They mobilize more completely the energies, devotion, and competences of men than do any other unremunerated forms or spheres of activity. In all of these ways, sects have much to tell us about the social order and about those things in which, but for the opportunity for this type of voluntary involvement, the wider society would itself be deficient.

5

New Religious Movements: Convergences and Contrasts

Decay and renewal in religion
There is a tendency for all established and traditional religions to institutionalize their arrangements, and for their activities and relationships to become ossified. This process appears to arise because of an evident tendency of men in all settled cultures to legitimize their procedures by reference to the past. Tradition becomes the touchstone, ensuring the wisdom and safety of particular arrangements. Clearly, tradition is associated socially with the dominance of the older people, and older people usually manifest respect, and perhaps even reverence, for the past. Until relatively recent times most, if not all, human societies, ordered their affairs with reference to the past; only in this century have societies come to organize themselves principally with regard to the present and, increasingly, the future. In traditional societies, the will of the gods was received from the past; in contemporary societies, the will of men is projected into the future, in what we call economic and social planning.

The ossification of religious teachings and practices was very much facilitated by the tendency for religion to be in the hands of specialists; religious functionaries were perhaps the earliest specialists in any department of life. These religious functionaries who claimed, more or less successfully, a monopoly of access to the supernatural, were élites, and they preserved from the past the wisdom which the society felt that it needed. Often they were the guardians of special shrines, the custodians of traditional truths, some of which they might keep as special secret knowledge or practice. Their business was to keep the truth pure, to maintain the sacred free from profanation, from corrupt ideas, unpurified persons, or desecrating activities. These functionaries, priests and sometimes lawyers, served the people—by providing reassurances; interpreting oracles; performing rituals; judging cases; pronouncing on the divine word or the divine law; specifying appropriate social relationships, and interpersonal and inter-group obligations; and interceding with the supernatural for the benefit of men. But they also tended to develop, as part of their élite status, a conception of religious truth which often transcended the understanding available to laymen, and the teachings they propounded were often arcane, abstruse, and, if erudite, sometimes also recondite and obscure.

In such circumstances, there has often been the likelihood that the religious truths and activities that were once propounded for the benefit of laymen—for the generality of the people—might become too remote from their everyday circumstances and experiences, becoming the exclusive, specialist, concern of the élites. And this circumstance has been one in which traditional religion has left itself open to challenge, since man's demand for salvation, for present reassurance, is recurrent and ubiquitous. Laymen seek assurances, counsel, advice, intercession, or ritual performances, from priests. If these are not forthcoming in terms acceptable to the laity, and with sufficient psychological force, then laymen may cease to support priests with their tributes and offerings. Since priests live off the surplus which farmers, fishermen, and other productive workers provide, there is a limit to the extent to which religious élites can ignore lay demands. Yet, often, what priests have developed as religious service has failed to satisfy laymen, and particularly so when religious teachings become obscure, and the conditions for salvation too remote. Then laymen seek recourse to alternative sources of reassurance, and to other avenues to the supernatural. The recrudescence of magic in many societies is an instance of such alternative resource to which laymen turn when they find the services of priests inadequate. Thus one finds in Theravada Buddhism the frequent employment of astrologers and herbalists who offer more proximate reassurance than is available from the remote soteriological scheme of Theravada Buddhism.[1] One finds the

---

[1] The phenomenon is well documented; see, for example, Michael M. Ames, 'Magical Animism and Buddhism: A Structural Analysis of the Sinhalese Religious System', *Journal of Asian Studies*, XXIII (June, 1964), pp. 21–52; Richard F. Gombrich, *Precept and Practice: Traditional Buddhism in the Rural Highlands of Ceylon*, Oxford: Clarendon Press, 1971; Melford E. Spiro, *Buddhism and Society: A Great Tradition and its Burmese Vicissitudes*, London: Allen and Unwin, 1971.

penetration of magic in Tibetan Buddhism, so that laymen have something other than recondite religious discourse as a source of comfort.[2]

In Christianity, the case has been somewhat different, even though indigenous magic persisted until relatively recent times in parts of Christendom. The Christian Church sought to eliminate all alternative sources of supernatural support, and so, when its theologians became too intellectualized, and made salvation too remote for the layman, the laity had recourse not so much to magical practices, but to new religious movements. These movements—heresies and sects in the eyes of officials of the established church—reinterpreted the message of Christianity, and very often made the specific offer of a more proximate salvation than that proffered by the Church. Such offers were sometimes ill-advised, and particularly so in the case of prophecies which fixed dates for an early second advent of Christ, accompanied by the destruction of existing social order in a cataclysmic battle, with the emergence of a new and perfect kingdom of God to follow.[3]

Other movements, however, gave rise to reformations of Christianity itself, with a radical re-examination of the premises on which established procedures had been justified. Frequently, such movements led to reappraisals of just what was the essential and original doctrine, and what were the subsequent embellishments and elaborations; what came from the inspired sources, and what had been added subsequently, perhaps in the interests of the priests as a class, or as a defence-mechanism for the church itself. Thus, Protestantism swept away not only many dubious teachings and practices concerning the Virgin Mary, for which there was no scriptural warrant;

[2] See Robert B. Ekvall, *Religious Observances in Tibet: Patterns and Functions*, Chicago: University of Chicago Press, 1964.

[3] There is an extensive literature on millennial movements. For the Reformation period, see George H. Williams, *The Radical Reformation*, London: Weidenfeld and Nicolson, 1962; for the eighteenth and nineteenth centuries, see, for England, J. F. C. Harrison, *The Second Coming: Popular Millenarianism, 1780–1850*, London: Routledge, 1979; W. H. Oliver, *Prophets and Millennialists: The Uses of Biblical Prophecy in England from the 1790s to the 1840s*, Auckland N.Z.: Auckland University Press, 1978; for the United States, see Whitney R. Cross, *The Burned-Over District: The Social and Intellectual History of Enthusiastic Religion in Western New York State, 1800–1850*, Ithaca, N.Y.: Cornell University Press, 1950; Ernest R. Sandeen, *The Roots of Fundamentalism: British and American Millenarianism*, Chicago: University of Chicago Press, 1970; Timothy P. Weber, *Living in the Shadow of the Second Coming: American Premillennialism 1875–1925*, New York: Oxford University Press, 1979.

but also the systems of 'dispensations' from the penalties of sin, by which the Church comforted the rich and earned money for itself; the influence of relics and shrines; and the whole apparatus of sacerdotalism, together with the requirement that the priests be celibate. Similar reform movements might be pointed to in the history of Japanese Buddhism, of course. I mention these developments, however, merely to indicate that new religious movements have risen in previous ages, and from the circumstance of their earlier emergence, we may learn something of the significance of such movements generally.

What new movements often offer is a revitalization of religious culture, sometimes by purging the established and ossified religious system of accretions, and sometimes by restoring things lost by attrition. A common feature of new movements is the emphasis on a more clearly determined scheme of salvation. It cannot be said that all new movements make salvation more widely available, but there have been many movements which have done just that. New religious movements often promise men more rapid spiritual mobility, and better prospects of salvation. They tend to make shorter and less recondite the training of priests, and sometimes they dispense with priestly functions altogether. They tend to simplify doctrine, to increase lay participation in ritual, and to make public even the secret teachings of the past. They may legitimize short-cuts in learning, and often they encourage education for the laity in matters that were once the specialist concern of priests.[4]

If this has been a general tendency of new religious movements in all past ages, we should expect to find the same characteristics in the new movements in contemporary society. An adequate assessment of modern new movements would demand examination of the social context in which those movements emerge. The characteristics of social structure undoubtedly influence the character of new religious move-

[4] The tendency for new movements to enhance the role of the laity and to facilitate their more rapid spiritual mobility, opening to many men functions that were, in older religious traditions, reserved to priests, and opening them after shorter and less recondite processes of training, may be observed in widely different movements, from West African cults such as Tigari (on which see J. B. Christensen, 'The Tigari Cult of West Africa', *Papers of the Michigan Academy of Science, Arts, and Letters*, XXXIX, Part IV (1954), pp. 389–98), to successive movements within Protestantism, from Lutheranism, through Moravianism, Methodism, to Brethrenism. Similar tendencies may also be observed, for instance, in Soka Gakkai.

ments, which arise in a situation when men are experiencing new conditions and new anxieties. Since religion always seeks to address human anxiety, so new movements are conditioned by the anxieties felt at the time of their emergence. These anxieties, in so far as they are new and not merely recurrent, stem directly from the changing character of social organization. We may ask, then, what it is about contemporary society that renders the traditional manifestations of religion inadequate to cope with human needs in the contemporary social context.

Religious decay in modern society
First, we must recognize that social organization has changed from its erstwhile communal structure and its profound localism to a societal system.[5] A society is a large-scale, internally coherent system of complex institutions which today is principally organized in the nation state. Men no longer live their lives in the context of one on-going social group, into which they are born, in which they live, and in which they die, and which has a sense of its own identity as a group even though its entire composition changes in the course of one long lifetime. Such communities included the dead as well as the living, and the dead continued to exercise certain constraints. In this century, because societal concerns have been rationally organized, because of the growth of communications, and particularly through the mass media, life is no longer lived nearly so exclusively or so intensely at local level. The vision and range of experience of the individual is immeasurably widened. Alien ideas, products and organizations all become part of every day life. Whilst it is difficult for the individual to see himself in direct relation to the wider world, none the less it is also hard for him to think of himself and his purposes without taking cognizance of the facts of that wider world that are daily borne in upon him. When events in remote places affect daily living and daily lifestyle, then local interpretations of relationships with the supernatural necessarily undergo transformation. Even though

[5] The process briefly sketched here is a central preoccupation of sociological concern, as found in the early works of Ferdinand Toennies, Emile Durkheim, and Max Weber. For important aspects as exemplied by more recent writers, see, for example, Robert Nisbet, *The Quest for Community*, New York: Oxford University Press, 1953; Jacques Ellul, *The Technological Society*, New York: Vintage, 1960; Arnold Gehlen, *Urmench und Spätkultur*, Bonn, Atheneum, 1956; idem, *Man in the Age of Technology*, New York: Columbia University Press, 1980.

religion is always marked by continuities with the past, the circumstances, of contemporary society make evident the fact that new interpretations of the super-empirical must take into account the widened horizons of the ordinary man.

Among the specific elements of contemporary society to which religious orientations must adjust is the availability of new techniques. Technical criteria determine an increasing range of social activities. They affect the extent and frequency of the individual's movement in the world—as a commuter who moves daily; as a tourist who moves annually or biannually to remote places; as a career man, whose work takes him to this branch, then to that branch of his company's business; and even, impersonally, as a television-viewer. Such movement brings him into contact with innumerable unknown, and therefore to him anonymous, persons. Other people are merely 'drivers' or 'pedestrians'; 'officials' or 'personnel'; 'assistants' or 'agents'—defined by their roles and not by their personalities. New techniques penetrate our relationships even with those whom we do know personally: the telephone, the feeding-bottle; and, most intimate of all, modern birth-control techniques. As a consequence of the new technical and rational organization, local distinctions, family peculiarities, even regional traditions, are set at a discount. Just as, in the Napoleonic era in Europe, the multiplicity of local standards, weights and measures, currencies, traditional arrangements were all swept aside to make way for new standards, so in our time, new technology is eroding yet further personal foibles, local neighbourhoods and the distinctive traditions and idiosyncrasies of all social units, groups, and individuals.

Contemporary society has acquired an ethos quite different from that of the societies in which the established traditional religions arose. To mention only the most obvious aspects of this ethos, we see that today the ideology of quality and democracy is everywhere canvassed, and in considerable measure implemented. The old pattern of authority that prevailed, not only in politics, but in social relationships, is increasingly at a discount. The idea of every individual making up his own mind within a certain range of choice, at least with respect to political and religious preferences, and in some measure with regard to personal life-style, interests, hobbies, and the use of leisure time, is the accepted ideal of our age. Obviously, religion in this context must function differently, must offer very different facilities, and must emphasize a type of relationship for believers other than that which was appropriate to traditional religious systems.

The age balance of status in society has also shifted—from old age increasingly to youth, a process more fully developed in the West than in Japan, perhaps, but evident in a measure even in countries with strong cultural continuities. The association is clear: whereas the old represented the past and its received wisdom, youth represents the future and its planned prospects. The growing dominance of the young in western societies is associated with the dependence on new techniques, rational procedures, and future orientation, and this has profound consequences for traditional culture and traditional morality. The old rules of society had been built up largely to protect the elderly, and they had been forged in the light of the experience that men gained in a lifetime. The young, however, suffer less from the absence of rules, and esteem them less. They can make their way in conditions of social chaos, and put social order at much less of a premium. Because the young are advantaged in learning new techniques, it is easily, but falsely, assumed that they are equally competent in the sphere of interpersonal relationships. The prestige of youth, in its association with new developments, in a world which prizes new technology, carries over, quite irrationally, to the moral sphere. Because the technical competence of older people is superseded it is fallaciously assumed that their moral wisdom is also superseded. Hence old wisdom is put at a discount, and the ethos of a youth-oriented society is that of every one 'doing his own thing'.

This free-wheeling sense of freedom in the moral sphere has profound social consequences, and it is perhaps to the issue of personal responsibility, and the attempt to find new paths to social order, that the new religious movements particularly address themselves.[6] For we have a curious hiatus between the apparent freedoms from the old moral controls associated, especially in the work sphere, and the constraints imposed by the new technological order itself. Whilst technology has freed men from the arbitrariness of ancient and perhaps anomalous

---

[6] See, on the process of moral change, C. H. and W. M. Whiteley, *The Permissive Morality*, London: Methuen, 1964; and its implications in the field of delinquency, Patricia Morgan, *Delinquent Fantasies*, London: Temple Smith, 1978.

local custom, it has imprisoned them within a new set of exacting obligations and demands. And these new constraints appear, in large part, so much less humane than those of the past; for, whereas the old morality was mediated by known persons, who could buffer the exactions of custom by human concern and sympathy, in the new situation the law behaves with impersonal coldness, and often with a new and quite arbitrary force, conditioned by statistical procedures, computers, and other inhuman, and often inhumane, apparatus. Society becomes increasingly abrasive, and sensitivity, moral awareness of each other, and interpersonal caring concern is given less place in the conduct of our affairs.[7]

The ethos of modern society is clearly unconducive to the maintenance of older religious patterns. We can see, at a less abstract level, how the conditions for the conduct of religious activity have changed. Let me simply enumerate some of the more obvious developments. First, there has been a massive expansion of education throughout contemporary society. Whereas education used to be largely concerned with religious teachings and moral wisdom, increasingly education has become technical, abstract, and scientific—and this has occurred even in those branches of learning that we call 'the humanities'. The development of the 'social sciencies' alone illustrates the extent to which the old approach—the approach of literature, history, and cultural appreciation—has been superseded by the positivistic, statistically-oriented, technical approach of modern economics and sociology. The consequences of such a development are a growing reliance on different sources of information, and a disparagement of traditional religious teaching. It is not only that scientific perspectives often conflict with those of the older religions, but that even where they do not, science seeks to put in precise, objective form what was often represented in vague, emotive religious language. Science commands prestige, and its formulations offer themselves for testing, and this willingness of science to be empirically tested, immensely adds to its plausibility. Thus there is a growing prestige differential between science and religion, and there is also an increasingly disproportionate command of resources. Science is thought to produce wealth.

[7] Some aspects of this problem are dealt with in Bryan R. Wilson, *The Youth Culture and the Universities*, London: Faber, 1970.

But whatever men believe themselves to gain from religion, those gains are much less easily represented in quantifiable terms. In a world in which quantification is vital, traditional religion suffers yet again.

Second, the world has been effectively internationalized in many respects. Ideas flow from one culture to another and this produces a new relativism in men's thinking. Religions that once appeared to comprehend the truths of the universe, and to be applicable to all mankind, are now seen to have been much more regionally conditioned, and much more dependent on particular social structures. Once men have some conception of the diversity of human history, what was once regarded as absolute religious truth is seen as truth relative to particular cultures. The consequence is an unsettling of traditional religious faith. Just as ancient religions were not couched in language that coped with the contemporary secular world, so they were not adapted to any cultural conditions but those of the societies in which they grew or to which they were successfully and slowly transplanted. In the past, the great religions spread slowly, migrating from the society of origin to other cultures. There was a slow process of cultural diffusion, in which a foreign faith gradually managed to grow in a strange cultural soil, till it made itself a part of that scene. Today, alien religions are known about, but they are known 'in the abstract', as alien intellectual systems. Those who come to know about them acquire little feel for them as such, but know about them intellectually and know about the social context of their origin. They are accepted relative to the time and conditions of their birth, not as systems of absolute truth. The result is a relativization that in some respect diminishes the claims of all alien religions, and, by extension, induces doubt about indigenous traditions.

To make a third of the many points that are relevant to a discussion of the contemporary context in which old religions seek to survive, it is clear that religion suffers from the almost explosive growth of the mass media. Once, religious instruction and religiously-inspired tales were the principal stuff of communication. Communications were communal and personal, and knowledge came in the context of unchallenged religious apprehensions of the world from known and trusted counsellors. Today, information pours forth impersonally on the widest variety of subjects. The appetite for information expands, and the relevance of what is learned, or heard, to any central religious conception of things is something which the individual must decide for himself. Most of the information and entertainment is secular, and religious ideas are pushed into the background. Even the style of communication affects religion. Traditionally religion was acquired from known members of the community; its substance, its style, and the circumstance of its diffusion entailed interpersonal trust, moral responsibility, and communal concern. None of these things obtain in the mass communications industry, which operates with very little moral responsibility, and with no personal or communal concern, and the style of which is alien to the core concerns of religious communication. But increasingly the mass media become the model of what communication is to be like: they provide a style which cannot be challenged. They establish a form which quickly becomes a norm. Children learn it and imitate it, and the significance of personal communications, and of moral sense in communicating, is lost—and this, among other things, must set traditional religion at a discount.

Since this is the social context in which old religions now operate, their decay in the modern world can well be understood. They fight an uneven struggle with forces and influences which characterize contemporary society, and which make of it an alien environment for traditional religion. Nor, for a variety of reasons, do ancient religions easily adapt to change of social circumstance. We have already mentioned the tendency for religion to sacralize the incidental accretions to its pristine message, for vested interests to arise, for expedient procedures to become matters of sacred necessity, and so on. Thus, to divest old religion of inessentials is a painful task for the custodians of those religions to undertake for themselves. One sees how, at present, the Roman Catholic Church, in its attempt at modernization, is riven with conflict about what is essential, and what are merely traditional incidentals to the faith. Above all, the problem arises because religion has legitimized its teachings, practices, and institutions by reference to the past, almost as if the past itself were a sacred entity. For traditional religions, the past is not easily surrendered. The language of the past, even if it fails to communicate much now; the symbols of the past, even though they have lost social resonance; past institutions, even though their structures have become incongruous to modern needs—all these, because of the nature of tradition legitimation, are inextricably bound into the style and stance of these religions; their excision would run the risk of rending the fabric of faith with profound destructive consequences.[8]

The openings for new movements
New religious movements offer reassurance to men in more immediate ways. They cut through the encumbrances of tradition; they use contemporary language and symbols, and a more direct path of spiritual mobility. In particular, they may employ methods that are rationally devised. There is, of course, a tension between religion and rationality, which relates to the super-empirical character of religious ends, to the fact that religion always espouses certain substantive goals, and, for their attainment, prescribes particular means (arbitrary means as viewed from the strictly rational viewpoint). Religion, too, operates in a personal idiom, dealing in interpersonal trust, communal goodwill, fellowship, the stimulation and diffusion of love for others. Rational criteria of efficiency are not its determining principles of operation. In consequence, there must always be unease when religions seek to rationalize their procedures. Yet, new religions have the opportunity in considerable measure to adapt the rational techniques to their own ends. They can do so in particular with respect to the non-worshipful activities in which they necessarily engage (and in competing with secular agencies that are also seeking to gain a clientele). Thus, they can be rational with respect to fund-raising, recruitment, publishing their message, office organization, and ancillary activities.[9] They may go so far as to institute regulated procedures for occasions even of private worship, as did the Methodists. Yet, they must carefully avoid the appearance of making efficiency an end in itself, of becoming too preoccupied with purely instrumental issues, occasioning a deflection of goals from the higher purposes of the movement to the intrinsic problems of organization *per se.*

[8] On this general problem, particularly as it affects religious traditions, see David Martin, *The Breaking of the Image*, Oxford: Blackwell, 1980.

[9] For a discussion of the adoption of rational techniques in new religious movements, see Bryan R. Wilson, 'American Religious Sects in Europe', in C. W. E. Bigsby (ed.), *Superculture: American Popular Culture and Europe*, London: Elek, 1975.

It appears to me that Soka Gakkai has been effective in the methods of rational deployment of personnel in the process of recruitment of members. In the modern world, paradoxically, because of the growth of bureaucratic organizations in the state and in industry, personal contact becomes something that is more highly prized than it was in traditional society in which all relationships were personal relationships. In stimulating its members to make personal contacts, to maintain some responsibility towards outsiders who are brought in, Soka Gakkai takes appropriate advantage of a modern need, whilst simultaneously conforming to older Japanese cultural patterns, in invoking the lines of respect that obtain in Japanese society between initiates and those who advise and guide them. Jehovah's Witnesses in the West have used a similar approach, of emphasizing the responsibility of all members to work to recruit others. They have deployed their members rationally, with effective coverage of territory to ensure maximum opportunity for everyone in a given area to learn at regular intervals about the movement. In the West, a new movement like the Witnesses cannot invoke a cultural disposition to respect teachers and guides to the same extent, but there are often ties of particular affection between newcomers and those who have instructed them in the rudiments of the movement's teachings.[10]

That new movements tend to be lay movements is also an adjustment to a changed social ethos. Traditional societies were societies with extensive systems of pronounced status differentials, and the claims of a sacerdotal class or caste to status superiority was an effective bulwarking of religious authority and power. Modern societies operate with much less difference between status groups, and such status differences as persist tend increasingly to be contingent upon differences of wealth, and more particularly of income. Religious movements cannot normally expect to offer their full-time personnel very high stipends, and, certainly in Britain, the salaries of the clergy have now fallen to levels below those obtained by various types of manual worker. It is thus clear that claims to distinctive status are not only contrary to the prevailing ethos of contemporary society, but, in countries such as Britain, would also be

---

[10] On Jehovah's Witnesses, see James A. Beckford, *The Trumpet of Prophecy*, Oxford: Blackwell, 1975; and *Social Compass*, XXIV, 1 (1977), entire issue.

incommensurate with the stipendiary possibilities of religious functionaries in our time. The new movements abandon these special status claims and employ lay personnel, and in the contemporary ethos, this gesture of normality fits the egalitarian assumptions of the times, and better facilitates the operation of a new religion than would the establishment of a sacerdotal caste.

In these respects, new religious movements adjust to the commanding ethos of contemporary society. But these new movements, as fundamentally religious movements, devote themselves to the timeless preoccupations of religion. Accommodating to new conditions, they may, none the less, not lose sight of the basic functions of religion. If one were to review a wide range of contemporary new movements internationally one might delineate a long continuum, at one end those which had maintained most fully the central concerns of traditional religion, to those, at the other, which had espoused the modern most extensively. Among the former would be many fundamentalist Christian groups, including most of the Jesus movements that developed out of the hippy sub-culture in the United States in the early 1970s.[11] Among the latter would be Scientology, with its bureaucratic type of organization, its modern psychotherapeutic practice, its emphasis on coursework, research, and its endorsement of the values of the contemporary secular world.[12] Failure to embrace modern techniques puts a religious movement at a disadvantage relative to the secular agencies with which it has to compete. On the other hand, too complete an espousal of modernity must for any movement put into jeopardy its basic religious concerns. Whilst new movements have the advantage of being able to adopt modern facilities and to utilize rational and technological procedures, they must do so with circumspection if they are not to sacrifice explicitly religious functions.

Religion in the past solemnized men's social relationships and

[11] On the Jesus movements, see Robert S. Ellwood, Jr., *One Way: The Jesus Movement and Its Meaning*, Englewood Cliffs, N.J.: Prentice-Hall, 1973; D. W. Petersen and A. L. Mauss, 'The Cross and the Commune: An Interpretation of the Jesus Movement' in C. Y. Glock (ed.), *Religion in Sociological Perspective*, Belmont, California: Wadsworth, 1973, pp. 261–79.
[12] See Roy Wallis, *The Road to Total Freedom: A Sociological Analysis of Scientology*, London: Heinemann, 1976.

their community life. In the modern world, natural community has largely disappeared: men no longer live, learn, work, play, marry, and die in the same community. Yet there is no doubt that men hanker after the benefits of community, seek contexts in which they are personally known, and in which they share responsibilities with others. New religious movements can supply precisely this context in a way that no other social agency can do. Other activities—politics, economics, even recreation— are dominated by specific interests and exchange relationships; only the family shares with religion the idea of the community as an end in itself, and the modern family, now nucleated, is too small to fulfil the functions of a community. Because religious activity is predicated on transcendental concepts, because sharing and caring are the core of its operation, because the celebration of the transcendent truth is also a celebration of the community in which the truth is cherished—for all of these reasons, religious groups provide the intrinsic, as well as the symbolic, benefits of community.

The new movements, even if they are international in scope and immense in numbers, operate at local level, bringing together local groups which become living communities in their shared identity. Even if, in their working life, people are obliged to go their separate ways, strong religious commitment draws them together for a wide variety of other concerns which men who do not belong to a religious group tend to pursue separately and in isolation. Thus, the members of a new movement tend to take up similar attitudes to politics, to recreation, to education, to illness, and towards outsiders and the outside society. Their religion may indeed itself prescribe certain general orientations to these matters. The essential point, however, is that religion again assumes a presidency over many aspects of life, colouring people's attitudes and establishing and reinforcing the links that bind men together. Obviously, in such communities, the opportunities for mutual help, for the exercise of disinterested love, for the distribution of relative status (which, after all, is basically social esteem), and the opportunities for a measure of authority and responsibility in the spirit of disinterested goodwill, all function to give people a sense of worthwhile commitment and personal belonging.

In traditional social life, when the community was the normal form of association, many of these benefits were experienced as an intrinsic part of life. Religion served to reinforce these benefits and to solemnize them, but they arose from the prevailing conditions and the existing structure. In the modern world, most men cannot naturally obtain these benefits, and this is particularly so for those who live in urban societies (although, even in the remaining rural areas, there has been a process of the urbanization of facilities and attitudes which has undermined community organization). Today, if these functions are to be fulfilled, that fulfilment must come from religious organization, and perhaps only new religious movements can provide it. Old religions lack the organization and the impetus, and often those who belong to them, even if devout, belong in an essentially conservative and sometimes lethargic spirit. It is in the new movements that there is a mobilization of active concern, and the maintenance of energetic commitment, from which the re-creation of community can arise.

New religious movements, then, may take on more responsibility than has been necessary for any religion explicitly to accept in the past, since they may take on the whole burden of community maintenance. To this task they can judiciously employ the new techniques available in advanced society and so find it possible to express more emphatic goals, make more overt and perhaps more programmatic commitment to the attainment of specific goals than was ever either necessary or possible for traditional religion. The new movements become, paradoxically, given the fact that they rarely embrace more than a minority of the population even in their countries of origin, more encompassing of men's concerns than were the older religions of the same tradition. In part, the very fact of lay organization and the background of a certain radical egalitarianism and democracy affect this posture, making shared participation of all members a more acceptable and, indeed, a more desired arrangement. Thus the house-group meetings, the Zadankai of Soka Gakkai, the stake organization of the Mormons, the hoza system of Rissho Kosei-kai and the Bible-study of Jehovah's Witnesses, are all examples of the way in which personal concerns can be set in the context of religious teaching and religious counsel. Such organizations become support groups, which people who are involved in the impersonal abrasiveness of modern society may find attractive and sustaining for their daily life activities.

The generational appeal of new religions

It is perhaps this encompassing quality of some new movements which enables them to appeal effectively to all age groups. Given the degree of separation between the generations in modern society, this is a remarkable accomplishment. Age groups become separate partly because of the very speed of social change and technical development, which creates a hiatus in cultural transmission, and causes a failure of moral communication. In contemporary society, the young come to regard morality—any system of ethical norms—as somewhat old-fashioned. For many young people, problems of any kind have technical and rational solutions (even though, in reality, moral problems admit of no such technical solutions). The older religions and the moral and social systems which they support and the assumptions of which are built into their thought and practice, appear, to the young, to be less relevant to the needs of everyday life as they know it. The new religions, and particularly those that develop from within a continuing indigenous tradition, appear to combine the possibility of preserving elements that are familiar and well-understood from the past, together with a style of presentation and a mode of organization which effectively makes that cultural inheritance a living thing in the present. The old find familiar ideas, and the young find concerns that are comprehensible in the modern world. Within a given society, new movements which stem from an older tradition, sprouting like new saplings from a root that has supported an older, and perhaps now partly decayed, trunk, may combine these divergent sources of appeal. These new movements become adaptations to the times of what appears as a timelessly true message which has its origins far back in the historical culture. The case is as well exemplified by the Methodists in the late eighteenth and early nineteenth centuries in England, as by some of the contemporary new religions of Japan.

Clearly, there are problems in this pattern of accommodation. Because a movement has adapted itself to modern forms, it may be viewed by older and more traditional people as a dangerous source of innovation, whilst, because it has old roots, it may be regarded, especially by some of the young, as a manifestation of conservatism, if not of reaction. There is even a time-dimension to these attitudes: new movements which shock conservative older people with their radicalism, and which appear to them to be betraying much of the past in the innovations that they make and the concessions that they offer, may, after twenty, thirty, or forty years appear conservative, because they have become repositories of so much past tradition—the tradition, or the elements of tradition, which they have themselves preserved.[13] It might be that some of the older among the contemporary new religions of Japan display exactly this type of life-course. A movement cannot, of course, afford to be too sensitive to these types of reaction by the outside world, and the diversity of judgement may itself indicate that a *via media* has been found, at least for the short time span. It must also be clear that in contemporary society, no religious movement can expect to be other than a source of contention.

Given the heightened differentiation in the social experience of older and younger people in contemporary society, however, it would be surprising were all contemporary new religious movements capable of making an appeal to all age groups. As the modern family has declined in size and in the duration of its intense associations, so, at least in the West, the assumption that a family would be united within one religion has been eroded. In largely secular cultures, most families maintain only nominal and perfunctory commitment to religion, and so it becomes easier for religious diversity to occur even within the family, and most markedly along the lines of generational divisions. Many of the new movements in the West are cultural imports which offer a redevelopment of the traditional wisdom of some society other than those in which these movements are active. Since these movements owe little to the indigenous tradition, the likelihood that they might appeal to older people in slender. Conversely, because they present an unknown, perhaps partly mysterious, and certainly exotic, wisdom from another culture, they attract the young. This is all the more pronounced when the culture from which they arise is one that has not been so much affected by contemporary technological development as have western nations and Japan. That fact alone gives these religions the appearance of standing closer to some arcane and ancient source of truth that has not been sullied by man's

---

[13] This is the case with the Peyote religion among North American Indians, for example; see the discussion in Bryan R. Wilson, *Magic and the Millennium*, London: Heinemann, 1973, pp. 435 ff.

interference with nature, or by the gross materialism and hedonism of advanced society, or with its corrupt policies, military entanglements, and power-madness.

The constituency in the West of many of these movements, of the Divine Light Mission, the Krishna Consciousness movement, the Healthy, Happy, Holy Organization of Yogi Bhajan, and the Unification Church, among others, is predominantly young people.[14] These are movements which (with the exception of the Unification Church, which claims to be a Christian organization) draw on very little if any of the indigenous tradition, and have little appeal for older and middle-aged people. Religious movements that draw adherents mainly from one generation tend to have a distinctive style and distinctive problems. In general, the public at large has acquired a negative impression of all of these movements, and this has partly arisen from the particular section of the population that they have recruited. Young people's movements have generally tended to be viewed with suspicion by the not-so-young, and the contemporary movements followed in the wake of a period of youth unrest which alarmed the press and public throughout the western world. A distinctive youth culture had arisen, and distinctive anti-social and aggressive styles had been disseminated among the younger generation. The counter culture, which was initially secular in both its style and concerns, was, for some young people, both moderated and legitimized by the acquisition, in the late 1960s, of a religious life-style and religious rhetoric. It was among the dissident youth culture that both the Jesus movement and the Krishna Consciousness organization looked for their recruits, the one gradually easing the path of return to the dominant society of the erstwhile wayward young, and the other by claimining to perpetuate the ecstasy of the counter-culture. For many older people, the new movements were tainted from their beginnings

---

[14] On the Divine Light Mission, see James V. Downton Jr., *Sacred Journeys: The Conversion of Young Americans to Divine Light Mission*, New York: Columbia University Press, 1979; on Krishna Consciousness, see J. Stillson Judah, *Hare Krishna and the Counterculture*, New York: Wiley, 1974; on the Healthy-Happy-Holy Organization, see Alan Tobey, 'The Summer Solstice of the Healthy-Happy-Holy Organization', in C. Y. Glock and R. N. Bellah (eds.), *The New Religious Consciousness*, Berkeley: University of California Press, 1976, pp. 5–30; on the Unification Church, see Eileen Barker, 'Who'd be a Moonie?' in B. R. Wilson (ed.), *The Social Impact of the New Religious Movements*, New York: The Rose of Sharon Press, 1981.

by the backwash of hippy culture, youth rebellion, and counter-cultural ideas. With adherents who were young and enthusiastic, and so able to communicate best with others of their own generation, these new movements set themselves out to draw in a clientele that was increasingly disproportionately drawn from one age stratum. The negative image which these groups created for themselves with the general public was exacerbated when parents discovered that their children had become converts of religions that were to them incomprehensible in aim and utterly alien in style. Much as some parents resented their children becoming hippies, at least as hippies those children were living lives transparently of their own choosing; when they joined the religious movements, many parents believed that their children had been abducted and 'brainwashed' to believe these strange and binding ideologies. Whereas the hippy life had been loose and transient, the new religions were apparently tight in their control and permanent in their demands. Since they were readily identified as persisting organizations, with leaders, policies, and techniques for proselytizing and fund-raising, they were easy targets for an outraged older generation. They could be condemned as sinister and predatory. Whereas hippies, disapproved as they were, were merely individuals who adopted a certain life-style, the new religions were available for attack because they were identifiable organizations. Those young people who chose to belong could be represented as 'victims' of the manipulations of the 'organizers'. Part, at least, of the strength of the hostility towards these movements appears to have arisen precisely because they capitalized on and reinforced the existing generational divisions in society.

Indigenous renewal in the West
In contrast with the animosity engendered by the new religions imported from the East, which, in their diversity and in the speed of their diffusion, constitute a phenomenon of an entirely new kind, new developments within the indigenous Christian traditions of the West occasioned less attention. In general, the Christian churches have engendered little that is new in many decades, except in a destructive sense, in the abandonment of old liturgies and the adoption, by way of replacement for them, of casual performances which imitate the ephemeral fashions of

the entertainment industry of secular western society. The congeries of movements known as 'the Jesus movement' arose among disenchanted hippies, and after a relatively brief period of extravagant emotionalism, relatively quickly returned its following into the general stream of evangelical Protestantism. Its excesses were initially condemned, but, except that it adopted contemporary styles and experimented in communal organization, the Jesus People were well within the confines of what might be called the revivalistic tradition of American evangelicalism. Only one or two offshoots—the most prominent being the Children of God—displayed any capacity for growth away from the pre-existing traditions of indigenous religion.[15] The one other, and much more significant, creative development in modern Christianity, has been the somewhat amorphous movement known as Charismatic Renewal.

Charismatic Renewal is a reassertion of the validity of what are known as the gifts of Pentecost, the principal of which is the capacity to 'speak in unknown tongues', which is to say, the capacity to give voice to unintelligible utterances in ecstatic moments of prayer, at what is believed to be the prompting of the Holy Spirit. This particular element in Christianity was for centuries condemned by the churches when it occurred spasmodically in enthusiastic revival movements. The gifts were officially held to have been withdrawn from Christians. For a long time, the practice of speaking in tongues was associated with heresy, but in the twentieth century the Pentecostal tradition burgeoned into a number of sectarian movements which, if not regarded as heretical, were certainly looked upon with disdain.[16] The informal style, casual procedures, abandonment of an ordered liturgy, and the ordination of their own ministry, were all disapproved by orthodox Christians. Since the end of the 1950s, however, the same manifestations of the 'power of the Spirit' have occurred within the Catholic, Anglican, Presbyterian, and other major denominations, and although the new Charismatics have not separated themselves to form a distinct organization, their frequent exercise of their spiritual faculties has led to the growth of a new style of worship

[15] On the Children of God, see Roy Wallis, 'Observations on the Children of God', *Sociological Review*, 24, 4 (1976), pp. 807–29.

[16] On Pentecostalism, see C. B. Cutten, *Speaking with Tongues Historically and Psychologically Considered*, New Haven: Yale University Press, 1927; Walter J. Hollenweger, *The Pentecostals*, London: SCM Press, 1972.

within the churches, even though many churchmen do not approve.[17]

This movement owes much to the prevailing ethos of western societies. Although its members continue in their membership of the orthodox churches, Charismatics come together in small informal prayer groups in which a democratic and egalitarian ethos constitutes relationships. There is open opportunity to all to participate and contribute to proceedings, and, at least in these gatherings, the formality, ceremonial, and solemn liturgical performance of church services are set aside. The emphases are similar to those that increasingly prevail in the secular culture. The style is informal, at times almost breezy. Implicitly, in the idea that God speaks directly to and through the individual believer to the gathered community, there is a strong anti-cultural and anti-authority orientation. Spontaneity is the watchword, and with it there is an accompanying commitment to immediacy and ecstasy. Emotional experience is virtually taken as a guarantee of authenticity. The intellectual traditions of Christianity, and the whole apparatus by which doctrine was formulated and transmitted, are set aside for the sake of direct experience. All of these characteristics appear to have been powerfully present in the youth culture of the 1960s and more widely in the general currents of anti-cultural and anti-establishment movements. Charismatics are not drawn exclusively from young people, nor even from among those who consciously entertained counter-cultural values, and yet this new movement, with a considerable contingent of middle-class votaries, as well as of priests and nuns among its members, manifests, perhaps with little awareness of the implications of the attitudes they espouse, much of the dissident and restless spirit and the rejection of formal procedures, dignity, order, and intellectual commitment that, in the last two decades, have so strongly characterized secular society in the West. The wider implications of the movement are that religious worship may be conducted just as effectively—and perhaps more effectively and more 'authentically'—without the service of priests or professional ministers, since, God, Charismatics believe, speaks directly to men and through them. Even though few Charismatics appear to be fully aware of these anti-structural

[17] On Charismatic Renewal, see Richard Quebedeaux, *The New Charismatics*, New York: Doubleday, 1976.

implications of their movement, its effects, both on the church organization and activities and on the wider society, may be no less profound for that.

Diversity in style and function
In remaining within existing church fellowships, and in recruiting followers from all age groups, the Charismatics differ significantly from the majority of new movements that have burgeoned in the western world. They exemplify the fragmentation of traditional religion from within, just as the success of the movements imported from other societies represent the erosion of traditional religion from without. Nor has the phenomenon been confined to either the western world or even to the advanced nations. In the third world, too, in South Africa, Kenya, Latin America, and the Caribbean, a similar process of the fragmentation of religious tradition has occurred, and even Islamic societies have not been entirely immune.[18] There are today, in most of these countries, many more new religions than have ever co-existed at any previous period of history, and these movements manifest widely divergent orientations, even though they share certain basic functions for adherents, and also share a claim to provide special and privileged access to the supernatural. There are, however, distinct differences to be noted, not only between individual movements, but also between generic types, and perhaps also between the types of movement that flourish in one particular society, say Japan, and those that flourish in another, say the United States.

We have already noted that in the West many of these movements, and certainly most of those which have exhibited most rapid growth, which have established themselves as organizationally separate and distinct bodies, and which have exotic origins, are movements that appeal specifically to the young. In general, these movements have demanded very high and even ascetic commitment from those who join, and particularly has this been the case in the early stages of their development. At that stage, with high ideals, bold claims, unrealistic expectations bolstered by rapid growth, these

---

[18] For an account of new movements in the third world and their social consequences, see Bryan R. Wilson, *Magic and the Millennium: Religious Movements of Protest among Tribal and Third-World Peoples*, London: Heinemann, 1973.

movements make strong demands on adherents, including, in some cases, the demand that they abandon all their erstwhile associations and activities, and, in a few well-known cases, that they commit themselves to a communal life-style. Such rigour is difficult to sustain, and since many of these communally-organized movements are dependent on the wider society for their economic resources (by soliciting gifts, selling produce, or by sending their people out into the wider world to work, or to collect unemployment payments), and perhaps also at times for social and moral support, eventually they may acknowledge the advantages of differential commitment among their following. That is to say, they sometimes adopt a somewhat relaxed pattern of demands on certain classes of adherent. The process is familiar in older sects—the new religious movements of earlier times. Thus even in sects such as Jehovah's Witnesses, which are in many ways so very different from the new movements being here considered (Krishna Consciousness, the Divine Light Mission, the Unification Church, among others), differential commitment is well institutionalized. The elderly Witness cannot really be a 'publisher' canvassing from door to door, and so he is excused what for others is a normal demand of membership; there are also 'pioneers' who often take only part-time jobs in order to be free to spend more time on such canvassing, and there are 'special pioneers' who devote themselves full-time for very small incomes, to missionary, organizational, printing or productive work for the movement. When such patterns exist among older and long surviving sects, we should expect that newer movements, if they are to survive, might also have need of such strategies, and this is indeed the case in exotic movements such as Divine Light Mission and the Unification Church, in such radical Christian groups as the Children of God, and in the rationally-oriented Church of Scientology. The pristine vision of a totally and equally dedicated fellowship necessarily recedes in the face of the exigencies of survival over the longer time-scale.

Despite the compromise implied in the acceptance of differential commitment among members, several of the new movements in the West have adopted the demand for an ascetic personal ethic. In this they reveal a perhaps surprising similarity with the indigenous evangelical tradition in Christianity, within which many of the new religious movements of the foregoing two centuries arose. There are, however, significant differences between the old evangelical Christian tradition of asceticism and that of the new movements. Within the evangelical Christian movements, whilst there was always a strong emphasis on the individual's personal need for salvation, which was to be attested by his moral comportment, his moral behaviour was also regarded both as an example to others and as in itself a contribution to social well-being. Evangelicals sought to impose their standards of morality on the whole society, and the dedicated evangelical took as a command relating to his personal moral comportment the injunction to 'so let your light shine among men'. The result was the diffusion of elevated moral standards. In the new movements, however, the demand for moral rigour and asceticism, whilst also of importance for the individual, is basically for the movement rather than for the wider society, towards which the movement is indifferent when it is not hostile.[19] Discipline is a pattern of self-control which provides coherence for the group, and this is especially necessary when the movement espouses a communitarian polity.

The new religions in the West have generally remained unconcerned with the wider society, seeking neither to influence its moral standards nor interfering in public policies. In this, they have differed from the much larger and more successful new religions of Japan. Western movements have had little to say on such issues as ecology, race, sex discrimination, armaments and nuclear power, welfare economics, and the responsibility of commercial concerns for their products—all of which are subjects on which the new religions of Japan have felt free to voice their concern. In this respect, the new movements of the West reveal the position which they share with evangelical movements, and stand in contrast to the trends within the secular society in which the mass media, the entertainment industry, advertising and even—when it pays— big business, all encourage the extension of permissive moral attitudes. Secular morality in the West reveals diminished interest in personal comportment, but there are increasingly vociferous pressure groups which seek to make the type of public issues mentioned above into specifically moral, or politico-

---

[19] For a discussion of this point, see Bryan R. Wilson, *Contemporary Transformations of Religion*, Oxford: Oxford University Press, 1976.

moral concerns. These groups are not, however, the new religions.

In Japan, in contrast, the new movements have become very much aware of the dangers of modern political policies, and make peace and pollution central issues of public and politic morality. The stance of the new religions in Japan may arise from particular cultural and structural characteristics of Japanese society, and since there may be few other large voluntary bodies with an independent voice, it may fall to new religious movements to fill this vacuum. In the West, the new imported faiths have been essentially preoccupied with the individual problems of their adherents and in promising personal benefits to them, while the various Christian groups have maintained their now traditional apolitical stance in public matters. Perhaps, in Japan, the issues of personal morality find reinforcement from other than strictly religious sources; in a much more homogeneous culture than that enjoyed by any western nation, moral comportment attains a far higher general standard without the need for religiously reinforced moral suasions. The problems of Japanese society, reflecting perhaps the dramatic impact of the last war and of the experience of atomic warfare, relate much more explicitly to the overt political currents of national and international politics. If these are widely felt conscious issues, it is understandable that the new religions in Japan should seek to come to terms with them.

The new religions of Japan have thus assumed social functions that remain quite beyond the various new sects flourishing among young people in the West.[20] These large new agencies have assume the role of what might be called 'mediating structures' in Japanese society, operating for large constituencies in the social space that exists between isolated individuals and the ultimate authority of the state. In the rapid processes of urbanization, industrialization, and technologization, individuals lost the security of the extended family group and of the local community to a very considerable extent. They have become more isolated and more anonymous in the vastly developed city. In the vacuum left by the old, local, district, neighbourhood, and regional affiliations that men enjoyed

[20] For a general discussion, see Fujio Ikado, *The Religious Background of Japanese Culture*, Tokyo: Association for International Education in Japan, 1973.

when society was more traditionally and rurally organized, there has been room for new organizations to grow, within which individuals might acquire a sense of belonging, and again experience the benefits of community—this time of the community of the like-minded rather than the community of the clan or neighbourhood group.[21] Because they operate through interpersonal connections, these agencies maintain a special sense of moral integrity, sustaining the high levels of moral commitment that men knew in the old intimate associations of the past. These agencies become the inter-mediate associations which sustain a level of moral consensus, in the manner in which Durkheim envisaged for renewed guild organizations.[22] But they do more than Durkheim imagined: renewed guilds would have been bound ultimately to material interests and economic concerns. For effective new agencies to arise in the modern state, it was necessary that they should command allegiance at a higher level of value consensus than would be afforded merely by shared economic interests. The one focus from which men might be mobilized for the expression and dissemination of such high-level values is clearly that of religion, through which disinterested goodwill might be elici-ted, and a diffused sense of altruism, moral commitment, and moral concern might be designated both as an explicit goal and as a latent consequence of wider saliency.

Such a task appears to be one that would now be beyond the strictly traditional religious organization of Japan. If such intermediate agencies were to operate, then, they had to be not only religious, but religion organized in a new form and with a message adapted to the modern world. The basis of such movements, if they were to revitalize moral, civic, and social life, could be neither explicitly political nor economic—nor was there a social base for associations with these wider aims and concerns except in the like-mindedness and the value-orientations of movements summoned into being with an explicitly religious *raison d'etre*. For them, economic welfare and politico-moral concerns became by-products—albeit by-

---

[21] The general conditions come out very clearly in recent studies, for example in Kiyomi Morioka, *Religion in Changing Japanese Society*, Tokyo: University of Tokyo Press, 1975; and in Robert J. Smith, *Ancestor Worship in Contemporary Japan*, Stanford, California: Stanford University Press, 1974.

[22] This issue is discussed in Emile Durkheim, *Professional Ethics and Civic Morals* (translated by Cornelia Brookfield), London: Routledge, 1957.

products of considerable importance among the latent social functions of the new religions in Japan. As agencies with extensive concern for the wider humanitarian issues, these new movements moved into a social vacuum in a rapidly developing society in which old forms of association have been outmoded or rendered defunct.

The Japanese case, with its extremely large, successful, and indeed powerful, new religions, obviously differs markedly from that of the West, where the new movements are both small and peripheral to the wider society. The Japanese new religions draw on indigenous traditions, and appeal to a wide spectrum of the public—much as the historical new religious movements of Christianity were able to do in the nineteenth century. The contemporary new movements of the West reflect the extensive and enlarging pluralism of western countries, and in some degree—since some of them diffuse philosophies and ideologies that are quite alien to the host societies in which they operate—they enhance that sense of cultural diversity. They represent a special facet of the modern facility for free choice in everyday life in such matters as the use of private leisure time, in contrast to the constraints of traditional culture. Such freedom, however, implies the growing loss of cultural coherence, and the fact of choice in such matters as religion and recreation indicates the indifference with which even ultimate values are regarded in contemporary society.

If our study of new religions produces no unified theory to explain, under one set of theoretical propositions, all such phenomena, wherever they are found, we need not regard such a conclusion with alarm. It is a sociological bias—and an unwarranted bias—to suppose that comparative analysis should always lead to unified theory and universally valid formulations. Such a conclusion can be produced only by ignoring the importance of empirical evidence and the historical diversity of societies and their cultures, and only by subsuming factually diverse contents under highly abstract summary propositions which obscure by their abstraction as much as they illuminate about social reality. New religions throughout the world undoubtedly have some features and functions in common, but they also manifest manifold differences, and the parts which they play in different societies are likely to differ as much as do those societies themselves.

6

Secularization and its Discontents

The thesis outlined

Secularization is a word which, for sociologists, is as much a concept as a mere descriptive term. The phrase, *the secularization thesis*, denotes a set of propositions, often loosely stated, which amount almost to a body of theory concerning processes of social change that occur over an unspecified period of historical time. Obviously, the details of such processes might be set out in varying degrees of specificity, and in application to different historical epochs. My concern is fundamentally with the recent past of advanced western society, but the thesis itself implies that there are processes of society 'becoming more secular' which extend backward in time over the long course of human history, and which have occurred intermittently, and with varying incidence and rapidity. It is, perhaps, today scarcely necessary to say that, in describing such a process, the sociologist is not endorsing, much less advocating or encouraging, secularization. To put forward the secularization thesis as an explanation of what happens in society is not to be a secularist, nor to applaud secularity; it is only to document and to illustrate social change, and to organize that documentation into a general pattern which provides some explanatory apparatus for each individual instance.

Secularization is not only a change occurring *in* society, it is also a change *of* society in its basic organization. It is one of several concomitant processes of fundamental social change, even though it occurs in diverse ways and contexts. Some secularizing changes have been deliberate and conscious, as in the divestment of the power of religious agencies, or in the laicization of church properties—to describe which the term was originally used. Others, such as the gradual diminution of references to the supernatural in everyday life, have occurred with very little conscious stimulation (and here I would discount the influence of those secularists and humanists, and others who are ideologically committed to bringing a secular society into being, as having been no more than, at best, marginal to the momentum of the process of secularization).

Secularization relates to the diminution in the social significance of religion. Its application covers such things as, the sequestration by political powers of the property and facilities of religious agencies; the shift from religious to secular control of various of the erstwhile activities and functions of religion; the decline in the proportion of their time, energy, and resources which men devote to super-empirical concerns; the decay of religious institutions; the supplanting, in matters of behaviour, of religious precepts by demands that accord with strictly technical criteria; and the gradual replacement of a specifically religious consciousness (which might range from dependence on charms, rites, spells, or prayers, to a broadly spiritually-inspired ethical concern) by an empirical, rational, instrumental orientation; the abandonment of mythical, poetic, and artistic interpretations of nature and society in favour of matter-of-fact description and, with it, the rigorous separation of evaluative and emotive dispositions from cognitive and positivistic orientations.

These phenomena are likely to be causally linked, and yet they occur in varying order, and with different degrees of rapidity. In what measure, or in what priority they occur, is an empirical question for each specific case, and cannot be settled, *a priori*. The complexity of social life demands that allowance be made for innumerable contingent factors and an inextricable tissues of causes; but the impossibility of ever laying bare every causal influence in proper sequence should not occasion us to abandon our conception of broad social processes, reference to which at least offers us an interpretative comprehension of reality. If I may, for purposes of clarity, resort to a definition of secularization that I first used some years ago, and which I have found no reason to modify, let me say that, by the term *secularization*, I mean that process by which religious institutions, actions, and consciousness, lose their social significance.[1] What such a definition does *not* imply is that all men have acquired a

[1] This definition was first used in Bryan Wilson, *Religion in Secular Society*, London: Watts, 1966, p. xiv (Penguin edn., 1969, p. 14).

secularized consciousness. It does not even suggest that most individuals have relinquished all their interest in religion, even though that may be the case. It maintains no more than that religion ceases to be significant in the working of the social system. Clearly, that that should be so, may release many individuals from religious obligations and involvements that they might otherwise have found it necessary to sustain: religion's loss of social significance may cause men to gain psychological or individual independence of it, but that is a matter to be investigated, since there may be other non-religious constraints which operate to hold men to religious institutions or to persuade them to go through the motions of religious rituals. The definition that I have used is intended to cover any or all of the various applications of the concept that I have indicated above. We may see them as related phenomena, even if we cannot always state the terms of that relationship.

It is sometimes objected that the process implicit in the concept of secularization concedes at once the idea of an earlier condition of social life that was not secular, or that was at least much less secular than that of our own times. We can readily make that concession, even though it must be clear that by no means all men, even in the great ages of faith, were devoutly religious, and that, at the time of its most effective organization, the church in Europe, for example, was bedevilled by internal heresy and external heathenism, and by laxness, lassitude, and corruption. None the less, by most criteria, the social significance of religion for the conduct of human life was greater than than it is now.[2] If we go back to earlier times, the evidence becomes even more overwhelming. Simpler cultures, traditional societies, and past communities, as revealed by their archaeological remains, appear to have been profoundly preoccupied with the supernatural (even though they may not have distinguished it by that name). Simpler peoples appear to

---

[2] My use of the term *secularization* is clearly wider than that of many Christian commentators who, explicitly or implicitly, equate *secularization* with *dechristianization*. Their emotional involvement is often such that they go to considerable lengths to show that past ages were by no means as 'religious' (by which they mean 'Christian') as is commonly supposed. But paganism was usually more, rather than less, religious than Christianity, and heresy was usually more trenchant and enthusiastic than normal Christian belief, and even orthodox churchmen, including bishops and popes, were drenched in superstition. In so far as Christian discipline eventually reduced these motley manifestations of religious consciousness, Christianity itself must be seen as a secularizing agency, as Max Weber long ago suggested.

have taken cognizance of themselves, of their origins, social arrangements, and destiny, by reference to a projected sphere of the supernatural. Their ultimate concerns, expressed perhaps most cogently with regard to death, were super-empirical, and such ideas, beings, objects, or conditions, commanded solemn attention and perhaps dedication. Everyday life was deeply influenced, and sometimes completely organized, with respect to a realm of transcendental suppositions.

In traditional societies, too, we may observe that the largest buildings are those devoted to religious activities, or raised in the consciousness of transcendent realities; the code by which life is lived is largely given from a supposed supernatural source (or perhaps from several); the symbols and the badges of identity that people employ are at least augmented, where they are not totally supplied, by religious authorities; and the ultimate goals of a people are set forth in other-worldly terms that relate to spheres beyond the empirical experience or the total comprehension of anyone. The remnants of such pheno-mena are still about us of course, even in the most advanced nations, still summoning recognition and even regard, although they are no longer the commanding heights of the polity, the economy, or any other realm of social organization.

Secularization, then, is a long-term process occurring in human society. The actual patterns in which it is manifested are culturally and historically specific to each context and in accordance with the particular character of the conceptions of the supernatural that were previously entertained, and of the institutions in which they were enshrined. Let me, to bring us to consideration of contemporary western society, instance the variation that occurs with respect to institutional associations. In Sweden, where the church is virtually a department of state, and where it is supported by taxation, the church remains financially strong, even though attendance at services is phenomenally low. In Britain, where the association with the state persists in a somewhat more attenuated form, and where the church receives no public funding, attendances are not so low, but voluntary donations are very small. In the United States, where church and state are firmly separated, atten-dances are high, and giving is generous. What three such cases show is that the meaning that is attached to church-going and church-giving differs in different societies. A straight comparison of the appropriate statistics tells us nothing about secularization, unless we can interpret those statistics in the context of culture and history. Thus, in the United States, with its high immigrant and highly mobile population, churches have functioned as much more basic foci of community identity than has been their role in settled societies. Or, to take a different consideration into account, few observers doubt that the actual content of what goes on in the major churches in Britain is very much more 'religious' than what occurs in American churches; in America secularizing processes appear to have occurred *within* the church, so that although religious institutions persist, their specifically religious character has become steadily attenuated. What this implies, then, is that the indicators of secularization may be specific to particular cultures.[3]

The pace at which each aspect of secularization occurs is also subject to variation. Thus religious institutions (the hierarchy, the priesthood, the social organization, and the material plant) may continue little changed during a period in which there is profound change in general religious consciousness, as our many empty churches indicate. Sometimes slow change in one area induces a sudden change in others, as when, in the 1960s, so many priests abandoned their orders. Steady decay may also be briefly halted, and even temporarily reversed, as occurred in the first decade of the present century in a dramatic, if short-lived, revival in Wales. Revivals and new movements stimulate heightened religiosity, and, on a facile view, they might be invoked as evidence against the secularization thesis. But on closer appraisal, we see that each movement represents the diffusion of religious dispositions among a section of population previously religiously unsocialized. This type of popular movement, for example, early Methodism or Pentecostalism, mobilizes religious responses; but it also disciplines those responses, eradicates random superstitions, rationalizes understanding and commitment, and works for the steady reduction of immanentism. These movements eliminate sacerdotalism and minimize mystery. Eventually they provide a new education of the emotions. In the West, one can indeed trace the

3 For a wide-ranging discussion of the national variations in the general pattern of secularization, particularly in its political aspects, see David Martin, *A General Theory of Secularization*, Oxford: Blackwell, 1978.

course by which, in one movement after another, the religiosity of the masses has been steadily called to order by these unwitting vehicles of increased secularization. The social influence of each of these successive waves of religious revival evidenced decline, however, as one might see from a comparison of the social effects in Britain of Methodism, then later of Salvationism, at the turn of the century of Pentecostalism, and of Charismatic Renewal in recent decades.[4] In so saying, I do not imply that Methodism was more authentic than Salvationism, or Salvationism than Pentecostalism. Nor do I comment on the quality of the transformation of the lives of individuals drawn into these movements. I observe only that, in the context of a changing structure of society, the effects of revivalism become less socially significant; the institutions and organization of society, and the relationships among individuals, steadily become better insulated from the effects of religious enthusiasm.

The context of secularization

Secularization occurs in association with the process in which social organization itself changes from one that is communally-based to a societally-based system. Unfortunately for the clarity of discussion, the term 'society' has been used, not only by laymen, but also by sociologists, to refer to any permanent, bounded, and internally co-ordinated collectivity of human beings, whether it be the two hundred members of the Dobu tribe or the two hundred million members of the United States of America. A keystone of sociological analysis has long been the distinction between *Gemeinschaft* and *Gesellschaft*, between local

---

[4] There is an extensive literature on each of these movements. For a sample on Methodism, see John Kent, *The Age of Disunity*, London: Epworth Press, 1966; Robert Currie, *Methodism Divided*, London: Faber, 1968; K. S. Inglis, *Churches and the Working Classes in Victorian England*, London: Routledge, 1963; A. D. Gilbert, *Religion and Society in Industrial England*, London: Longmans, 1976; James Obelkevich, *Religion and Rural Society*, Oxford: Clarendon Press, 1976. On Salvationism, see Roland Robertson, 'The Salvation Army: The Persistence of Sectarianism', in B. R. Wilson (ed.), *Patterns of Sectarianism*, London: Heinemann, 1967, pp. 49–105. On Pentecostalism, see B. R. Wilson, *Sects and Society*, London: Heinemann, 1961 (reissued by Greenwood Press, Westport, Conn., 1978), pp. 1–118; and on Pentecostalism and Charismatic Renewal, see W. J. Hollenweger, *The Pentecostals*, London: SCM Press, 1972; John T. Nichol, *The Pentecostals*, Plainfield, N.J.: Logos International, 1966; Richard Quebedeaux, *The New Charismatics*, New York: Doubleday, 1976.

community and impersonal association.[5] If we take the community to be the persisting local, face-to-face group, as typically represented by the clan or the village, we may contrast it with the extensive, impersonal, politically co-ordinated state society. Western history, and perhaps history everywhere, documents the process by which local communities are fused into a wider system of relationships, the texture of which is not predominantly that of bonds between total persons, but that of bonds between role performers. Initially, the societal system may have been no more than the extension of uncertain political power, which affected local life only intermittently and in very limited respects. Increasingly, it has become the total co-ordination of local life into an extensive network, extending to every aspect of political, economic, judicial, educational and recreational activity. Local crafts, local products, local customs, local dialects have all shown a rapid diminution in our own times. The process by which so large a collectivity of communities and individuals are drawn into complex relationships of interdependence in which their role performances are rationally articulated is the process of *societalization*.[6] In this process, human life is increasingly enmeshed and organized, not locally but societally (that society being most evidently, but not uniquely, the nation state). A concomitant of that process of societalization, I suggest, is the process of secularization.

Put it in another way, religion may be said to have its source in, and to draw its strength from, the community, the local, persisting relationships of the relatively stable group. It is clear that religion may, in certain circumstances, be provided with a framework of a large-scale organization of relationships that transcend the local, regional, or national level, as no one concerned with the history of Christianity could forget. Yet such a structure is only the political apparatus acquired—in the case of Christianity, borrowed or inherited—from the secular

---

[5] The distinction is generally taken back to Ferdinand Toennies, *Gemeinschaft und Gesellschaft*, 1887 (English translation, *Community and Association*, by Charles P. Loomis, London: Routledge, 1955), but similar ideas are found in other writers, particularly Sir Henry Maine, *Ancient Law*, 1861. For a discussion, see Robert A. Nisbet, *The Sociological Tradition*, London: Heinemann, 1967.

[6] *Societalization* has not established itself as a regular term in sociological literature, but it appears to me to be necessary to distinguish the process by which large-scale, ongoing, internally co-ordinated, complex social systems are established, usually including, as a significant element, the process of state-formation.

sphere. In essentials, religion functions for individuals and communities, at its worst for a client, and at its best for a fellowship. Its votaries are served as total persons, not as role performers, and in the same spirit, the service demanded of them by their faith is that of earnest personal commitment.

The course of social development that has come, in recent times, to make the society, and not the community, the primary locus of the individual's life has shorn religion of its erstwhile function in the maintenance of social order and as a source of social knowledge. Of course, religion does not disappear: institutions survive, consciousness lingers, religious individuals and groups persist. New movements emerge, and often by presenting religion in a more demotic and rationalized form, attach large followings. Yet, whereas religion once entered into the very texture of community life, in modern society it operates only in interstitial places in the system. The assumptions on which modern social organization proceeds are secular assumptions. The processes of production and consumption; the co-ordination of activities; the agencies of control; the methods of transmission of knowledge, and its substance—all things that were once powerfully conditioned by religion—are in modern society all organized on practical, empirical, and rational prescriptions. Societal organization demands the mobilization of intellectual faculties; it contrasts with the desiderata of communal order, which depends, instead, on the mobilization and manipulation of affective dispositions. One might, then, juxtapose the two phenomena: the religious community and the secular society.

The salient differences between life in the community and life in the society may be set over against each other in terms that, if not themselves religious, carry with them connotations of religious commitment. Communal relations among total persons entail trust, loyalty, respect for seniority, and clear patterns of authority that build on biological determinants. Persons matter more than role, and goodwill more than performance. The society is based on impersonal role relationships, the co-ordination of skills, and essentially formal and contractual patterns of behaviour, in which personal virtue, as distinguished from role obligation, is of small consequence. Whereas, in the community, the individual's duties were underwritten by conceptions of a morality which was ultimately derived from supernatural sources, or which had reference to supernatural goals, in the society, duties and role performances are ultimately justified by the demands of a rational structure, in which skills are trained and competences certificated; roles are assigned and co-ordinated; rewards are computed; and times are measured and allocated.

Societal organization is itself the result of processes of rationalization, and clearly it takes time for a predominantly rational societal system to supersede the patterns of communal order. The system becomes more effectively rationalized as new techniques and planned procedures are adopted and in-stitutionalized. Technology, indeed, encapsulates rationality. The machine and the electronic device are supremely rational; every superfluous element of structure and function is elim-inated. Means are precisely related, as efficiently as possible, to properly specified, empirically testable, ends. The thrust is towards the eradication of the incidental, the whimsical, the wayward, the poetic, and the traditional. As a passing illustration, consider how our social equipment has become increasingly purely functional, increasingly cost effective. Until less than a century ago, all manner of utilitarian objects—from spades to houses and from boats to factories—were artistically embellished, often at considerable cost in time and effort. Aesthetic effort had social implications, and the ornamentation itself was often suffused with cultural and religious meaning. Controlled emotion—and it was often controlled by the invocation of directly religious concepts and symbols—was welded, sewn, painted or hewn into even the simplest, or even the most costly, of man's instruments and equipment. Man invested his emotion, his uncertainties, and his *joie de vivre* in the works of his hands, even when his products were primarily and essentially functional. His rational acts were shot through with what, from a strictly rational perspective, were entirely gratuitous accretions—customs and conventions, traditions and celebrations, artistry and invocations. The cult of functionalism in architecture and design has not become the vogue of modern society merely incidentally, as a random and transient artistic style. Rather, its dominance pays tribute to the logic of the rational, economic, and technological order, which increasingly presses its imperative demands on the form, content, style, and ethos of every branch of human activity. In rational artefacts, art becomes excrescence; traditions become waste of time; customs become anachronisms; rituals (divested of their emotional content) become routines; and, except in well-encapsulated areas, even creativity may be perceived as a potential threat to the regulated order on which the system depends, unless it can be tailored to rational need.

Rational precepts affect not only the economic system, and through it, the cultural sphere; they have powerfully affected the political organization of social life. The rationally constituted economy has been followed by the rationally constituted society, and this has increasingly become the conscious goal of modern states. Social functions are increasingly systematized. The consistent application of the criteria of cost efficiency would alone ensure the steady rationalization of administrative procedures throughout a state system. With ignorance or disregard of the often powerful latent functions which they fulfil, for such matters as a sense of identity or social cohesion, nor-rational elements, no matter what their antiquity, are not to be justified in the terms by which the system increasingly operates. Anything which impedes the thrust towards total rationalization induces pressure for its own elimination or diminution. Such pressure comes not from sinister, hard-faced, politically acute men who are in any way either *personally* animated or even intellectually well-formed, but from the imperatives of the system itself. Of course, a state system may be said to serve certain, necessarily arbitrary, ends, and these may be expressed in the form of political slogans— freedom, democracy, equality, and so on. In practice, the political tendency follows the economic in the compulsive and progressive further rationalization of the various departments of social life.

There are as yet untranscended limits for both economics and politics, of course: parts which rationality has not yet reached. These are such facts as those of human birth, ageing, and death, and so of the replacement throughout the systems of role players; of human emotion and its resistance to purely rational forms of control; and of the uncertainties of socialization. These phenomena must, as yet, be accommodated within the system as best they may, like the hills which stick out above, distort, and at points destroy the rationality of the grid system of streets in a city like San Francisco. But the thrust towards the elimination of all such impediments, for the rationalization of all social routes, is unmistakable, even though actual state societies manifest varying degrees of rationalization. A state that has slowly evolved, such as Britain, manifests less consistency of rationality—since historical residues persist—than do consciously-organized states like the United States and the Soviet Union. Even with rational constitutions, the irrationalities of social life remain, sometimes in dramatic example, as in the continuance of slavery in America long after equal freedom was constitutionally prescribed. That the best-laid plans for rational society are sometimes thwarted by the irrational is evident in the case of Belgium. And sometimes such plans may even be self-defeating as in the almost paralysing system of checks and balances built into the American legal system. Thus, from the perspective of the rational man, imperfections persist, but the direction, the impetus, and the urgency of the current process of social change can scarcely be gainsaid.

In any human society, the idea of the supernatural (in whatever form it takes) is an arbitrary presupposition. A wholly rational social structure would dispense, wherever possible, with items of this kind, since the implication of such a structure is that it should be entirely internally coherent and self-sustaining, making no recourse to any external source of legitimation. A modern state does not need a creation myth of the kind ubiquitous among tribal or communal peoples. In a nation-state, such a myth may persist, but it is as part of the ethnic identity of the nation, not in justification of the rational foundation of the state, that this type of ideological weapon is used. Much less, then, does a league of states, striving to form ever larger agglomerations, need such a device to symbolize unity and co-ordination. The creation myth of the new state, or the new league of states, is a document with articles, clauses, and provisions that are, in principle, amendable as, with every increase in rationality, the partners expect better to manage their incidental irrational consequences—their economic malfunctions, the lapses in social control, or the ineffectiveness of socialization in the distribution among the population of an adequate level of motivation. It is to rationally planned legislation that Britain turns to deal with its strike-prone workers and its football hooligans; or that the United States seeks to control drug abuse in its armed services; or that the Soviet Union tries to cope with widespread alcoholism.[7] Neither nation states nor the United Nations, nor even the European Community, need the mandate of heaven to legitimize their existence. They stand on the supposedly self-evident rationality of their respective political and economic purposes.

The collapse of community and custom

Religion, by which I mean the invocation of the supernatural, was the ideology of community. In every context of traditional life, we may see religious symbolism and religious performances used to celebrate and legitimate local life. There were religious procedures to protect the local settlement; there were super-natural agents to whom the family or the clan and its members could relate; by reference to religion men were reassured of their power, secured in their status, justified in their wealth, or consoled for their poverty. Religion could give the best guarantees of fertility for mankind and the abundance of the means of sustenance. It provided the means for according public recognition and identification to the young; for healing the sick; for inducing respect for the elderly; and for coping with bereavement. Its points of reference were to things local (some of which were, of course, also things universal). It built on the biological basis of relationship, and its language was often the language of the emotions, conspicuously so in Christianity, with its symbolism of father, brethren, mother, and child. In its higher forms at least, religion intimated an ethic for social comportment, provided the basis for shared moral expect-ations and moralizing exhortation.

All of these one-time functions of religion have declined in significance as human involvements have ceased to be primarily local, and as human associations have ceased to be communal. Industrial society needs no local gods, or local saints; no local nostrums, remedies, or points of reference. The means of sustenance are not local. Personal gain is the common sense of

[7] That non-rational, emotionally-oriented behaviour should persist, and should do so in so pathological a form, in an increasingly programmed society, should occasion us no surprise. The diminution of the careful, traditional processes of socialization by which individual demands for emotional gratification were gently disciplined, has led to extremes of repression and expression of the emotions which now characterize all technologized social systems.

modern life, needing no further legitimation, whilst material provision, not spiritual solace, is what society now offers to the poor. Fertility is no longer a positive virtue; it is to be thwarted rather than facilitated. Public recognition and identification are impossible for the vast majority, and men even enjoy their anonymity: in our large connurbations, people do not always know, and even more often do not care, in which borough they live, and have no notion of where its bounds might be beaten. Local life now needs no celebration: what is there to celebrate when the community that sleeps together is not the community that works together or plays together? Diurnal mobility and life in localities which demand demographic imbalance now become normal. Even the surrogate communities that are based on functioning groups such as the professional guilds, which do not take locality as their organizing principle, no longer seek religious legitimation for their distinctiveness. A pope may appoint a patron saint for, shall we say, bank managers or car dealers, but those occupations scarcely operate to any particular saintly maxims. As for the family, it is protected by insurances of a different kind from those laid up in heaven, and power, status, and wealth are no longer justified in the terms of the Christian conception of natural law. The idea that God ordered men's estates died perhaps not so long after Archdeacon Paley, and today men do not accept, but rather are encouraged to dispute, their claims to 'estates' (something that we now refer to as 'differentials'). So much the worse, then, for what, in the halcyon days, sociologists used to call 'value consensus'. Sickness today is only very marginally a matter for religious action, and, for them that mourn, funeral services today often appear less a source of comfort than an occasion for discomforture.

If the stable community declines because of the common pattern of diurnal mobility in the world of commuters; because of annual migrations, and tourism; because of the frequency with which careers demand that families move house; because of the separation of school from home, indeed the separation of everything which people now call 'life' from work; then what need is there for a child to be publicly received and initiated? What indeed, would he be initiated into, and what would be the effective way of doing it? When community is not a reality, initiation must be either a sentimental recollection or a travesty.

If divorce becomes increasingly the recognized way to term-
inate a marriage, as abortion terminates a pregnancy, then
the symbolism of baby, mother and father cease to have that
resonance of ultimate verities that, in settled communities, they
may once have had. We have learned to use different categories
with which to interpret social life, and these categories are not
emotionally resonant, particularistic symbols, but conceptualized abstractions, the purported generality and objectivity
of which are often backed by statistical indicators: such
categories are class, role, age-cohort, labour-unit. We develop
these new concepts to grasp the impersonal and rational order
which the old intimate symbolism could never comprehend.

The large-scale societal system does not rely, or seeks not to
rely, on a moral order, but rather, wherever possible, on
technical order. In this sort of social arrangement, much less
importance is attached to personal dispositions, to comformity
with a code of custom, to the education of the emotions, to the
processes of socializing the young into responsible humane
personal attitudes. After all, if, by time-and-motion studies,
data retrieval systems, credit-ratings, conveyor-belts, and
electronic eyes, we can regulate men's activities, and in
particular their vital economic functions, then why burden
ourselves with the harrowing, arduous, time-consuming weari-
ness of eliciting moral behaviour? Since the socialization of
children is so delicate a task, demanding all the balanced arts of
persuasion, sensitivity, refinement, courage, patience, and high
moral standards in the teachers themselves, why not, now that
we have such effective quasi-coercive techniques of social
control, cut short the process and rely on them? We go further.
We assume that if there are residual moral problems with which
technology and instrumental techniques cannot cope, then we
can legislate about them—as in codes on racial or sexual
discrimination. Where morality must persist, then it can be
politicized, and subject to the direct coercive force of the state.
As for purely personal morality, that quaint concept, so vital to
communities in the past, modern man might ask whether it had
not become redundant. In modern language, to be moral is to be
'uptight'; to express moral attitudes is to inhibit people when
they want—as modern men say that they have a right to want—
'to do their own thing'. To canvass the maintenance of public
morality, except in areas where morality can be politicized, is,

apparently, to favour censorship, constraint, or, in the opinion of some sociologists, to reveal that what one is really afraid of is of losing one's own precarious social status.[8]To espouse such a cause would be to set oneself in opposition to all the diverse forces of contemporary 'liberation'.

The balance of the communal order was struck in a personalized world that was part of a moral universe. The individual was involved in a society in which moral judgements were the basis of decisions, or purported so to be. To say this is not to say that those judgements were right, but only to indicate that this was the style of decision-making. The world was suffused with values, and the values often occluded the facts. In a societal system, such judgements cease to have relevance; custom, which was the code in which many such values were enshrined and given partial expression, falls into decay. It no longer services as a buffer zone, protecting men from the abrasiveness of the operation of the law; no longer operates to communicate a sense of rectitude and to state the terms in which men may enjoy the goodwill (or the ill-will) of their fellows. The society is underwritten by no such values, but by empirical facts and their rational co-ordination: what good is custom when we have discovered a faster, cheaper, quicker, way to go about things?

The traditional patterns of order were sustained by what, at their best, were shared intimations and apprehensions of the supernatural. The moral order was, ultimately, order derived from intimations (of whatever specific kind) of a super-empirical sphere. In the advanced societal system, the supernatural plays no part in the perceived, experienced, and instituted order. The environment is hostile to the super-empirical: it relies on rational, humanly-conceived, planned procedures, in the operation of which there is no room for extra-empirical propositions, or random inspirational intuitions.

---

[8] The thesis that moral crusades particularly attract those who suffer status insecurity has been developed by Joseph Gusfield, *Symbolic Crusade: Status, Politics, and the American Temperance Movement*, Urbana, Ill.: University of Illinois Press, 1963; and Louis Zurcher and R. George Kirkpatrick, *Citizens for Decency: Anti-Pornography Crusades as Status Defence*, Austin: University of Texas Press, 1976. This thesis, so thoroughly in the 'debunking' tradition of latent functionalism, might have crept into the popular sociological anti-authoritarian canon but for the incisive criticism of Roy Wallis, *Salvation and Protest*, London: Frances Pinter, 1979, esp. pp. 92–104.

The moral community and the rational society
The comparison that I have made between community and
society has been deliberately overdrawn. I have sharpened
differences to bring them out in higher relief, but I do not think
that I have distorted the tendencies. Obviously, in the
contemporary social world, the remnants of the community are
not yet extinct. The human will to sustain communal relationships and personal connections defies the bureaucratic structure
of the state, the unions, and big business.[9] The communally
organized past (the word 'organized' is, of course, itself an
anachronism) persists within the societally structured present.
But community has been severely weakened, and even intimate
relationships are now invaded by our dependence on technical
devices (for example, in such matters as birth control), and by
the constraints of rationally-ordered required performances.

In some respects, the community may appear to be more alive
than is actually the case, and this is so because of the persistence
of what might be called the rhetoric of community. No
association in the modern world is too impersonal, too
desiccated, too devoid of all human feeling for someone—
usually someone who is responsible for it—to find occasion to
describe it as a 'community'. Headmasters and Vice-
Chancellors so describe to conferences of freshmen the arid
concrete structures which they inhabit; politicians seek to evoke
emotional warmth by the use of the term for their faceless
bureaucracies; unions, with that mixture of nostalgia for the
common struggle of the past and the cynicism with which they
face the future, identify themselves as brotherhoods, and their
local organs as 'chapels'; and our new super-bureaucrats in the
Common Market call that agglomerate mass a 'family' of
peoples, a European 'community'. Such reversion to the
language of community in the interest of impersonal, rational
structures of society is dictated only because there appears to be
no other language in which to summon loyalties and goodwill,
on which residually (and herein lies a point of substance) even
rational systems must depend. The rhetoric should not deceive

---

[9] At times the will to defend community is compromised by the prevailing conception
of appropriate means. When, in 1966, the students at Berkeley set up a 'Committee to
establish community' they failed to see the paradox of using bureaucratic means (a
committee) to attain ends that could never be attained by planned procedures.
Community is not established, it is a natural growth for which the propitious conditions
had been destroyed—largely by the pervasiveness of planned procedures.

us. It does not relate to present realities, and it is used, misguidedly or cynically, only because, when goodwill is needed, for the occasion when sentiments are to be mobilized, the rational system has produced no other agency. In this lies, perhaps, the Achilles heel of the societal organization, which takes into account almost everything—everything except certain residual properties of humankind itself.

In overdrawing the contrast of community and society, I do not wish to appear to idealize the community of the past. Communities were not havens of morality: there were immoral men as much as there were moral exhortations, and the latter would not have been so necessary but for the former. There were defectors and there were miscreants. There was cruelty at local level, and there was periodic disorder. My concern is rather to indicate the assumptions on which such patterns of social life operated, put in as uncompromising a way as possible. It is morality as a basis of legitimacy that concerns me. It is in contrast to those assumptions of a moral order that I seek to contrast the implicit premisses on which repose the norms of the large-scale internally-coordinated system of advanced society.

The community—perforce—relied on the diffusion of moral sense, even though it did not escape coercion and forcible constraint. Modern society relies on an impersonal, fundamentally amoral rational order, although it, too, must invoke coercive force from time to time. Men were no more wholly moral in the community than they are wholly rational in the society; my concern is to expose the basis of legitimacy implicit in each system, albeit acknowledging that, in the contemporary everyday world, we all live at varying points between the two. Morality is not yet dead as a concept, and rationality has not yet gone so far as the pressures for calculable order may yet induce it to go.

It is not my purpose to extol the community at the expense of the society, nor to offer the moral code (whatever the content) as intrinsically superior to the rational system. Let us be clear: there are advantages, to which we are all accustomed, and on which we are dependent, in being treated impersonally, and in not being judged by, shall we say, the warts on our noses. Who among us wishes to give up the principles of abstract justice and the rule of law, or the formal equality of universal norms? The community, let us acknowledge, excluded as well as it included, discriminating in favour of its own, in terms of kinship, ethnicity, or locality: given the 'mixed society'— if I may coin a phrase analogous to the 'mixed economy'—in which we all live, with its still lingering elements of communal life, we may all of us feel, at certain times and in certain circumstances, that these forms of discrimination are desirable, or at least inevitable, since we have not yet entirely abandoned the sense of belonging that comes from kinship or nationality or linguistic group, or even locality. The value-judgements that we make with respect to these things will vary from individual to individual, from age-group to age-group, from class to class, and from lingering community to nascent interest association. My point, essentially, is that we cannot ignore the fact that these value-judgements are made, or that we appeal to divergent sources and assumptions of legitimacy in day-to-day issues as well as in the conduct of our public affairs. Nor can we ignore the tendency, so much on the increase in our own times, for communal norms to be overridden in favour of societal norms. There is an increasing displacement of the moral by the rational and the technical. The societal system relies less on people being good (according to the lights of the local community), and more on their being calculable, according to the requirements of the developing rational order. Thus it is that our discontents are more likely to focus on the values displaced than on the values not yet institutionalized, more likely to be a lament for the old moralities than an impatience for the new rationalities.

There is a sense in which both the morality of the community and the rationality of the society are both eligible to be described as 'value systems'. It is certainly possible to subscribe with deep feeling to rational values, as it is to a set of arbitrary, religiously-enjoined regulations about proper comportment and appropriate order. In practice, however, it appears that the old moral systems evinced an attachment and an affection less readily evoked among the generality of men for rational patterns of order. One has, of course, seen spirited and passionate appeals for the rule of law, for impersonal and impartial dealing, and yet, somewhere, there is a contradiction in the idea of a passionate appeal for the dispassionate: there is a point, when one is pleading for rational procedures, where passion has to stop. The form of justification has to be consonant with rational argument itself; proofs are assumed and reason is held to suffice to convince all 'right thinking' men capable of following the rules of logic. In contrast, the old moralities, the customs, and the traditions, are often enjoined with feelings which the rationalizer can scarcely comprehend. Used only to instrumental, cause-and-intended-effect thinking, he has no comprehension of the intrinsic feeling which custom and tradition engender, little awareness of the cluster of deep emotional investment in rules and forms that rely on such essentially human virtues as sensitivity, sympathy, respect, and reverence. Part of the difference relates, no doubt, to the fact that moral systems were often enjoined by specialized moral custodians, elders, or even professional exhorters (often a priesthood) who sought to elicit good behaviour, whereas rational procedures are assumed to be self-evident, not requiring any such special advocacy to provide a patina of sentiment for their essentially instrumental precepts.

The old moralities dealt substantially with matters of passion. They employed ideals of love, trust, loyalty, and patriotism: the emotions were close to the substantive virtues that were enjoined. Emile Durkheim, himself a rationalist, half-saw the problem when he demanded that in the new societal order, with its division of labour and its contingent dependence on the evolution of a system of professional ethics, men must be induced to love—not their local community, but the society. What he demanded was that the old emotional commitment, born in the community, should be transferred to the society—a society for which he sought to prescribe a rational ethic. He could not bring himself to suppose, committed as he was to reason, that reason alone would be enough: love, too, would necessarily be involved. Durkheim saw the problem of advanced society—that it would need goodwill, disinterested affection, if it were to work, but he did not adequately realize the extent to which the rational premises of the new order would destroy this attribute of the moral community.[10]

The old morality constituted a system of substantive values: the new rationality composes a system only of procedural

---

[10] Durkheim tells us repeatedly that morality begins where disinterestedness and devotion begin, and devotion must be to the collectivity. Because society is internalized in men, so they must love it and desire it. See his *Sociology and Philosophy* (English translation by D. F. Pocock), London: Cohen and West, 1953, pp. 56–7; also the discussion in *Professional Ethics and Civic Morals*, London: Routledge, 1957, esp. pp. 60–1, 70.

values. Rationality, after all, cannot determine among ends, but can only direct us not to entertain simultaneously ends that are mutually contradictory, and then to choose the most efficient means for the attainment of the ends we select. The values of the societal system are procedural values to an ever-increasing degree; ultimate ends, substantive commitments, are pushed back in an infinite regress in our concern to choose the best means for proximate ends, which themselves become the best means to yet further ends. Of course, some of the old substantive values still come into play, but the goals set forth in advanced societies tend to become increasingly abstract, and often subject to dispute. And we settle such disputes, where possible, on technical grounds, relying on the unity of technology and the formal rationality of bureaucracy to win sufficient assent to carry us on to the next set of issues. Our persisting disputes become matters, not of the clash of arbitrary loyalties (such as patriotism), but of men struggling about their different answers to the question, 'Rational for whom?' Thus, an example occurs when, in society's interests, new work techniques should be introduced, and old equipment, procedures, or mines should be phased out, but, when in the interests of particular sections of society—workers, managers, or miners—exactly contrary policies are demanded.

Yet there appears to be a persisting undercurrent, in modern society, of demand for values of a more positive, more substantive kind. At every turn, there is evidence of disenchantment with technology. It is easy to evoke nostalgia, and it is easy to deride it; but nostalgia must be seen as an important, if often also an impotent, social phenomenon—a measure of our disenchantment. There is growing concern about our systematic, rational destruction of our own environment, expressed in the group of issues that hide under the heading of the ecological. There is recurrent anguish about the loss of community and the eclipse of the sense of neighbourhood which is acute when people live and work in high-rise buildings, learn in large and increasingly centralized schools, and negotiate their lives in the impersonality of our cities. We resent the cost and condemn the inefficiency of what we call the 'caring services' which do so much less effectively what was once done by kinship groups and local communities. Perhaps, even on the criteria of technical efficiency, some of these new developments are less efficient than the communal structures that they displaced; and, beyond that, they may produce less immediate human satisfactions. And there may be longer-term consequences, that we have hardly as yet recognized, to add to our rationally calculated balance-sheets.

The nature of salvation

Beneath the surface of my comments on values and the community has been the issue of religion. Religion provided the legitimation of substantive values, arbitrary values, values taken on trust, by faith, as received intimations of how people might live. Those values were reinforced by the idea of devotion to some supernatural order which was meant to provide guidance for what men thought was the natural order, and what was, in fact, the social order. The decline of religion has been associated with changes in the received understanding of what is to be done, and the way in which such injunctions are legitimated. Perhaps no one religion encompassed the total framework of order, and some did so more fully than others. Perhaps one should think of successive religions, or successive revivals, as geological strata, overlying each other, and, at times, interpenetrating each other, and certainly it would be wrong to equate, for example, Christianity in the West with 'religion', particularly since Christianity itself, and especially in its Protestant form, was itself an agency of secularization, eliminating much of the previously established magic and mystery of the world. One must regard as 'religion' a wide variety of intimations about the supernatural and, in consequence, about the moral. Thus, religion is represented not only in formal theological systems, elaborate liturgies, or supernaturally sanctioned moral codes, but also in propositions which aver such things as that it is 'unlucky' for a child not to be baptized; that it is a violation of God's law to eat meat on Friday; or that one ought not to walk on gravestones or speak ill of the dead, for fear of the consequences that might ensure. These may be elements of folklore, but they are part of the apprehension of the supernatural that must be counted as religion.

Sociologists have generally accounted for the persistence of religion by reference to its latent functions; since, they believed, religion could be shown to be patently false in its manifest claims and assertions.[11] It was to unintended consequences that sociologists turned to provide explanations for the ubiquity of religion, and so religion was elevated—in the eyes of religionists for quite the wrong reasons—to a significant place in the social scheme of things, as sociologists saw it. Religion might not be true, but, for this functionalist school, it was certainly good—in fact it was indispensable. It established a focus for community loyalty; provided occasions for the expression of group cohesion; it supplied a basis for social control; it legitimated group activities, polities, and policies; it interpreted the cosmos; and it facilitated, and also regulated, the expression of appropriate emotion. These functions were conceived as 'social', but even where religious systems acquired, as did Christianity, an impressive political international presence, it could easily be shown that these functions necessarily operated primarily at local level, in the community, and, indeed, much of the functionalist analysis was based on anthropological data about relatively small tribes.[12]

But the process of societalization, as we have intimated elsewhere in these essays, has been a process in which latent functions have been made manifest, and so important is it to grasp the implications, that it is worth lightly retreading the ground with the phenomenon of secularization uppermost in mind, for men no longer rely on unintended consequences or incidental by-products for the ordering of social life. The emphasis has shifted to self-consciousness and management, programming, and planning. Cohesion is no longer expressed by shared adoration of symbols; the collectivities involved are now too big, and their backgrounds too diverse, and their knowledge too extensive and too fragmented, for a totem, or a god, a saviour, a virgin, or a saint, to convey much to them. 'Civil religion', so-called, is the feeble remnant of what remains of the latent functions of religion in providing social cohesion— and that is more the celebration of the institutionalizing of the state than of the birth of a nation. Who now believes in patriotism as a primary virtue? Once the local community dies,

---

[11] The argument followed here echoes in part that pursued above in Chapter 2, 'The Functions of Religion in Contemporary Society'.

[12] The tradition goes back to Emile Durkheim, *The Elementary Forms of the Religious Life* (1912), English translation by J. W. Swain, Glencoe, Ill.: The Free Press, 1954, which, following its development in the works of B. Malinowski and A. R. Radcliffe-Brown, came to influence American sociologists of the 1940s and 1950s.

so the sentiments that could once be extended to the linguistic group, or the nation state, also die. It is no accident that patriotism and nationalism today flourish only in the less developed societies, and among minorities that consider themselves to be politically oppressed. (Just at the time when the leading states of western Europe seek to sink their national identities for an economic gain, it is apparent that the Basques and the Bretons, the Scots and the Sardinians, the Catalans and the Welsh, assert their nationalism as never before.) Social control no longer depends on intimations of divine wrath, or on future punishments for present misdeeds, but on a battery of ever-growing laws, many of them more concerned with technical than with specifically moral matters. Social activities and political policies take little heed of divine will; even the Christian parties of continental Europe are, by virtue of their Christianity, no longer distinguishable from parties of any other kind. Religion no longer explains the world, much less the cosmos, and its explanations of social phenomena are utterly ignored; indeed, when Catholic or Anglican archbishops today wish to pronounce on social affairs they rely neither on revelation nor on holy writ. They set up commissions, often with considerable reliance on the advice of sociologists. Only with respect to the facilitation and regulation of the emotions are the latent functions of religion still evident, and then, usually, privately, and mostly for those who are marrying or mourning. More generally, modern society has different ways of summoning, and of silencing, emotional expression: the pop concert and the pop festival are the occasions for release (ideally in relatively hermetically-sealed enclaves); the mass media of simultaneous distribution, and especially television, are the agencies by which the emotions are numbed, and in which those who experience emotion are fairly effectively isolated from one another, and from a living social context.

Making latent functions manifest, and developing agencies to fulfil them is part of the process of rationalization. What I have contended above is that religion does not anywhere offer itself as the purveyor of latent or incidental benefits—indeed, that idea is virtually self-contradictory. Religion presents itself as the agency of manifest salvation, which, as we have already seen, may, whatever its cultural content, be summarized from a sociological perspective as present reassurance. Of course, the higher religions may not always have accurately perceived or defined the nature of the evil which men have felt or feared. Their tendency has always been to elevate, universalize, and ethicize soteriology. The difference between magic and religion is that the benefits and reassurances of religion remain spiritual, general, and abstract. Magic posits specific consequences and effects for particular action, and, but for the saving provision of self-fulfilling cautions, would expose itself to a possibility of pragmatic test. It offers more particular reassurance than that offered by the higher religions, but even so, the reassurance that even these higher religions dispense must, whatever the universalism of the terms in which it is offered, be locally available. Men have wanted salvation, that is reassurance, in their own communal context, and the experience of community life provided the conceptions and the substance of hopes for reassurance here or hereafter. However described, the substance of reassurance is drawn from lived experience and lived emotion—and that experience and those emotions have been forged in the local community.

Operative religion has, therefore, always found, if it were to succeed in convincing men that it could reassure them, that it must meet men's present needs as locally and communally experienced. This circumstance has imposed some strain on the higher religions, the etherealized and abstract concepts of which, so engaging to literati and specialists, quickly outdistanced the everyday understandings of ordinary people. So the great religions necessarily retained, and regularly reinvoked, for their laity, all those more specific and concrete promises of blessings which did not too much compromise the doctrinal coherence of their soteriological schemes. The anecdotes of healings and miracles, of simple faith, of material blessings, little as these have to do with the elevated ideals of salvation of theologians or commentators, had to be retained to encourage lay belief. Whatever the degree of abstract doctrinal coherence produced by scholars, it was always the plausible and indispensable functions of priests or counsellors for local laymen that enabled a religion to survive. The fact that intellectuals refined to subtle niceties the doctrines of the Christian Church, or that Buddhist exegetes have reconciled the Gotama's teachings with those of modern psychology and physics, should not obscure the fact that it was not these accomplishments, so much the creation of the schoolmen, which commended the faith to the vast majority of laymen. Similarly, the fact that Christianity inherited an administrative structure from an empire, or that historians have so closely followed the struggles of popes and kings, should not leave us unaware that the reality of religion has always resided in what it could do at local level in its effectiveness as an agency of reassurance.

Thus, against the ultimately secularizing thrust of ecclesiastical and intellectual rationalization, there persisted—as long as the immediate community was the dominant locale in which life was lived—a powerful, if in modern times diminishing, countervailing tendency. When doctrinal schemes grew too abstruse, and when salvation became too improbable or remote, or subject to conditions too rigorous for most laymen, as in a heaven reached only through aeons in purgatory, or a nirvana attainable only after thousands of rebirths, then laymen (and sometimes even monks) have come to demand a shorter cut and a swifter hope. They have turned to diviners, astrologers, healers, prophets, and messiahs, or they have behaved as if eternal bliss was much more immediately available directly after death. From a doctrinal point of view, one may say that such elevated scholasticism was always being corrupted by lay demands for better reassurance. In Theravada Buddhism, one saw the symbiosis effected between Buddhist monks in their temples, and astrologers and diviners at their gates, the latter being sometimes consulted by the former, or the monks even performing these magic arts themselves. In Mahayana Buddhism, one sees how Tantrist magic has penetrated the religious system, and how it is has been accommodated to it in various schools.[13] Folk religion and local magic persisted throughout the Christian world for centuries, and, in some nominally Roman Catholic Latin American countries, do so still. Men might go through the motions of accepting orthodoxy, but they may not always accept that orthodoxy is enough. The attitude is epitomized in the response of a

[13] See Richard Gombrich, *Precept and Practice: Traditional Buddhism in the Rural Highlands of Ceylon*, Oxford: Clarendon Press, 1971; G. Obeyesekere, 'Theodicy, Sin and Salvation in a Sociology of Buddhism', in E. R. Leach, *Dialectic in Practical Religion*, Cambridge: Cambridge University Press, 1968; Melford E. Spiro, *Buddhism and Society: A Great Tradition and its Burmese Vicissitudes*, London: Allen and Unwin, 1971; Robert B. Ekvall, *Religious Observances in Tibet: Patterns and Functions*, Chicago: University of Chicago Press, 1964.

nineteenth-century Lincolnshire farm worker who was asked by
the local Anglican clergyman why, although he came to the
Anglican church on Sunday mornings, he still consorted with
the Methodists at their chapel in the evenings. The parishioner
replied, 'We comes to church in the morning to please you, Sir,
but we goes to chapel at night to save our souls.'[14]

One might say, following Weber, that the diminution of local
cults and magical concerns, on the one hand, and the
intellectual development and centralized organization of religion, on the other, are themselves gestures in the direction of
secularization. The development, in church structure and
church doctrine, of hierarchy and system does not, in the nature
of religion, entirely displace the expectation that the supernatural should operate at the local level, but it does regulate and
circumscribe its local operation. The aids to salvation available
from the local priest or minister must be everywhere equally
efficacious, in all the higher religions; what a superior
functionary offers at a more central place can only supplement
the facility regularly available to all believers through their
local agencies. Yet, it is also vital to these higher religions that,
in so far as control can be exercised, there should be no random,
local manifestations of the miraculous (with only rare excep-
tions, themselves subject to central control).[15]

As doctrine and structure become centralized, hierarchized,
and increasingly well co-ordinated, so religious power is
conceived to operate essentially in formalized ways and through
specified channels. Immanentism gives way to transcendentalism, which leads to a further removal of supernatural power
from the lives of ordinary men in everyday situations. The world
is disenchanted. As long, however, as the locus of life was the
community, where the vast majority of men lived and died

[14] J. Obelkevich, op cit. p. 157.

[15] Even within Christianity, which, in its major denominations, is the most effectively
controlled and hierarchically co-ordinated of all religions, such centres of extraordinary
sacredness exist, most conspicuously as shrines evoking pilgrimage. Shrines, like relics,
sacred places and sacred objects, are remnants of magical, immanentist religion. In
Christianity they are integrated into a calendar and a terrestrial system of control: the
miraculous becomes delimited by the need for order. Often such phenomena are merely
tolerated, and scepticism persists among the faithful, and even among the hierarchy, but
they are concessions to local demand, which is the ultimate lifeblood of the faith. Some
localities, persons, objects, and seasons are permitted to claim exemplary virtuosity, as
stimulants to more general piety, but not as agencies that create any real differences in
the quality of salvation that must be everywhere locally available.

among known kinsfolk, clansfolk, and neighbours, there were always powerful impediments to the centralizing, intellectualizing, and secularizing tendencies. Local religion—now designated by urban man as the religion of the heath (heathen) or the village (pagan), and as 'superstition'—demanded that wherever official religion existed, it should compromise and temporize with local need. When, however, men ceased to live in communities, when their lives, or the lives of the vast majority, were lived out in impersonal and functionally specialized contexts, so the locale in which religion had flourished best ceased to provide it with hospitality. However contemptuous the priestly or intellectual classes might become about the religion of local communities, it was in these communities that the demand for religion had been most sustained, no matter that they were disposed to eclecticism, syncretism, and superstition. It is to the passing of natural communities, in which people lived virtually all their lives and undertook most of their activities, that we may look for a significant part of the explanation of secularization, when that term is used to refer to the transformation of religious consciousness.

The sources of our discontents

The modern social system leaves no space for a conception of ultimate salvation, any more than modern scientific anatomy leaves space for the individual soul. In so far as modern men might seek proximate salvation, their recourse must increasingly be to rational procedures institutionalized in the social system. Today, religious perceptions share an uneasy and shrinking frontier with rational precepts. To survive, the great religions have made many concessions to the demands of rationality, particularly in matters of organization. Within the ranks of traditional religion there are those who actively canvass, as the only prospect for success, the need to grasp modernity, to rationalize their own procedures, to reorganize and rebuild on the pattern of some secular institution, of which the army is a favourite model.[16] These radicals seek to divest faith of the time-honoured custom which had become the foil of its timeless truths. Much more vigorously, the new religions,

---

[16] For an example, concerning the Church of England, see Leslie Paul, *The Deployment and Payment of the Clergy*, London: Church Information Office, 1964, which consistently likened the church's operation to those of an army.

themselves less trammelled by tradition, have conjoined, in the dissemination of their message, modern and rational procedures with the substantive, arbitrary values of their specific religious message. Yet, even here, the latent tensions between faith and reason are not entirely obviated in the consciousness of individual believers. As everyday life in modern society demands ever extending commitment to rational procedures, so the personal, religiously-inspired caveats of the truly religious man are likely to become increasingly vestigial, and he the more likely to acquire a sense of his own marginality. Even the votary of a new religion, which conforms in so many external particulars to the demands of rational organization, may find himself attacked because somewhere at the core of his faith there are arbitary elements which, by the standards implicit in the social system, people readily declare to be obscurantist, irrational, emotional, or even magical.

Let me briefly exemplify the type of tension that persists between the divergent modes of consciousness, values, action, and relationship that derive respectively from religious and rational orientations to the world. Salvation is invariably mediated through personal relationships in the performance of action towards others, whether deities or humans. In Christianity, the saviour himself must be known as a person, and one's faith in him and one's behaviour towards one's fellow men are the basis on which one is to be judged. In Buddhism, despite the more abstract principles of a law by which men will be saved, obligation to others figures no less prominently, and even if, in doctrinal Buddhism, the concept of a personal deity is absent, none the less, there have been recurrent tendencies for deification, either of a particular Buddha or bodhisattva, or, in folk Buddhism, for the persistence of older gods, reverence for whom even the Gotama Buddha did not seek to suppress. These relationships, and the acts of charity, goodwill, and earnest soul-searching demand that the believer see himself in his religion not merely as a role-performer, but as a total, and totally committed, being. That demand stands in sharp contrast to the demands of modern life. In every activity—saving only certain kinship concerns—the individual merely plays a role: he is expected at any time to utilize only a narrow selection of his attributes and competences.

The expectation that commitment to religion should be a

total commitment is well exemplified in the case of the religious functionary—for instance, in the Christian priest or minister. His calling is presented as far more than a job or even a profession: it implies total loyalty to an ethic, an unending obligation to a way of life and to the values of faith. His work transcends all contractual commitments; it belongs to an ancient order, to relationships rooted in community. The criteria that apply to the religious calling are not those of efficiency, cost, speed, or co-ordination; they are not the concerns for the most cost-effective means to specified ends.[17] They are diffuse, and coterminous with all that is human. Thus, the implications of this calling could not be further removed from the considerations that dominate almost all other departments of modern life. For the minister of religion, men in themselves are ultimate ends, just as religious activity is an end in itself. Yet, in modern society, men are not ends-in-themselves: as role-performers, they become adjuncts to the machine, units of input in a system which matters more than they do. Their personal attributes, their sensitivity, their native dispositions, and their purely personal needs become irrelevant in their role-performance; men, in such a system, are merely the means. The antithesis between the religious conception of humankind and its responsibilities, and that of any modern social system (capitalist or communist) could not diverge more sharply.

The advanced technological society is, then, an inhospitable context for the religious *Weltanschauung*. Religious institutions compete on increasingly unfavourable terms with other agencies which seek to mobilize and manipulate men's resources of time, energy, and wealth. Those other agencies can employ, much more effectively than traditional religion, all the techniques of modern science and organization; they are unhindered by the types of impediment to the adoption of rational systematization that are found even in the new religions. Religious perceptions and goals, religiously-induced sensitivities, religiously-inspired morality, and religious socialization appear to be of no immediate relevance to the operation of the modern social system. For every social problem, whether of

[17] For a discussion of the clergyman's role, see Anthony Russell, *The Clerical Profession*, London: SPCK, 1980.

economy, polity, law, education, family relations, or recreation, the solutions proposed are not only non-religious, but solutions that depend on technical expertise and bureaucratic organization. Planning, not revelation; rational order, not inspiration; systematic routine, not charismatic or traditional action, are the imperatives in ever-widening arenas of public life.

Yet, as we have already seen, the rational system is not enough. If, by utilizing their specialist skills in cumulative order, men have built up a rational structure which is infinitely and more relentlessly rational than any one individual could ever be, yet, behind that rational order there lurk the discontents of men who look for something more. Irrational man inhabits rational society, the alien social context cumulatively produced by a refined division of labour which has extracted from each individual a rationally calculated role performance. The discontents of modern man have much to do with the sense of alienation that a rational order induces. The source of the lesion between background assumptions and mature experience is not far to seek. The basis on which the child is socialized depends on affective faculties that are unamenable to rational procedures. Men learn to cope with the world in terms of personal trust, parental love, personal intimacies, and local involvements; their early years are spent in a small, stable, community of intimate relationships and enduring affections. Traditionally, the world into which the child was socialized had strong continuities with the world in which the adult would live out the dispositions implanted in childhood—sometimes with the selfsame people. In the modern world, however, there are profound discontinuities between the situation of socialization and the impersonal contexts in which the individual will live out most of his life. The early training that is to draw forth human qualities for ordered personal relationships in later life become less congruous with the world that now exists. The moral and humane faculties that are implanted become muted and amended, and perhaps, in some respects, entirely replaced by the technical criteria of rational efficiency. Personal relationships grow less important than impersonal role-playing. Trust, once vested in people, comes to be reposed in systems and techniques.

And yet, without trust, without mutuality, with only reduced and fragile possibilities for enduring relationships, how will those minimal requirements of even the most rational system be met? Whence will come the civic consciousness, the detached goodwill without which even rational social systems cannot work? The process of societalization, which I believe brings secularization and demoralization, may threaten the continuity of those basic dispositions on which human society of any sort depends.

Anxieties about the social order are recrudescent preoccupations among mankind; history is a recurrent tale of older generations who bemoan the fact of change, the shift in mores, the breakdown of custom, and the growth of immorality. We must permit men to indulge in nostalgia and pessimism; we may discount something for age, since the elderly perhaps recall the normative structure better than they recall their early transgressions of it. And we must allow something for the normal unease which any process of change may induce. Beyond these concessions, however, we may perceive manifest disruptions occasioned by the processes of societalization and secularization. This unrest is of many kinds. It includes concern about demoralization and the breakdown of civic order in urban contexts more extensive and more intricately organized than any that ever before existed. It recognizes, and is alarmed by, new techniques of social control, public surveillance, and the invasion of privacy. It is fed by growing awareness of the exploitation and pollution of the natural environment, towards which man has lost his old sense of reverence. It responds to the knowledge that violence can be systematically organized on a scale hitherto unparalleled by governments and even by terrorists. It embraces widespread uncertainty caused by recurrent betrayals of democratic principles by subterfuge and corruption. Our modern discontents include all these matters that belong to the public domain. They also include our awareness of the changing quality of personal relations; the sense of loss of community life; the disenchantment that men feel when they recognize just how invasive of personal life have become the precepts that govern the market-place and the factory, and how much has been lost in human sensitivity. Our manifold and various discontents appear to lie in the disruption of those idealized conceptions of a normative order and a sense of transcendent goals and wider purposes, and the contexts in which these things acquired sustained meaning.

Traditional religion, in the West and in other fully modernized countries, has succumbed to the transformation of social organization. Nowhere in the modern world does traditional faith influence more than residually and incidentally the operation of society, or even, for the generality of men, the quality of everyday life experience. There are attempts to revivify religious life in the new religious movements, to create contexts in which impersonality and anonymity may be overcome, and in which something like community of feeling is, however briefly, restored. It is not surprising that so many new religions emphasize small groups, discussion meetings, communes, or cadres with strong principles of association among relatively small numbers. Their gatherings are often neither local nor long-sustained, but in the intensity of interaction they re-create some, at least, of the effects of community life. They seek a new synthesis between the universalism that became a powerful intellectual and rational orientation in the modernizing world, and the strength of localism, even if that localism merely re-creates the benefit of smallness of size without, usually, either the reinforcement of natural proximity of living or the totality of involvements that were shared in the local communities of the past.

Such endeavours are, as yet, and certainly so in the West, only marginal evidences of our discontents, and marginal attempts at their assuagement. It does not appear that men will be able to remake the world we have lost, and, unless there is a massive change of heart, a veritable revolution in thought and feeling, and a willing surrender of many of the conveniences of modern life and organization, it is difficult to see how the otherwise irrevocable pattern of societal order could be reinfused with religious inspiration. As yet, only at the margins and in the interstices, and principally in the domain of private life, has such religious endeavour been effective, in allowing some men, at least, to transcend the present discontents, and in producing, by way of the dissemination of dispositions of goodwill and commitment, that salt of the earth that is necessary to sustain the social order.

Index of Subjects

Index of Authors